TRIUMPH HOUSE

WHAT A WONDERFUL WORLD

Edited by Chris Walton

First published in Great Britain in 1996 by
TRIUMPH HOUSE
1 - 2 Wainman Road, Woodston,
Peterborough, PE2 7BU

HB ISBN 1 86161 002 5
SB ISBN 1 86161 007 6

Foreword

Over 200 Christian poets have come together to celebrate the beauty and enjoyment of God's wonderful world and the many colourful animals and flowers that adorn our pathways and brighten our days. Wherever we turn we can see God's Handiwork and throughout the seasons these amazing views change in ways that could not be copied by any human hands. These talented writers create pictures throughout the pages of this anthology as they take you away to a place of calmness and tranquillity.

This 'place' is reachable by anybody, and is free to enjoy. Open your door, step outside, and free your mind to this inspirational creativity.

Chris Walton
Editor

CONTENTS

GOD'S GIFTS

A brown sparrow in the green grass,
Hopping around for his food,
Beady eyes, bright as new glass,
He has to feed his brood.

Baby animals struggle to find
Their balance on wobbling legs,
Mother gives them a lift from behind,
As for milk their bleatings beg.

Little lambs with quivery tails,
Blind kittens nosing for nipple,
From new-born pups, tiny wails,
It all makes my blood warmly ripple.

The welcome in a child's eyes
When he sees his mother's face,
Is one of life's sweetest highs,
Other care it does all erase.

A sturdy roof over our heads,
The friendly glow of a fire,
Our hearts to the Lord are led,
To His love we truly aspire.

This marvellous world He created
I truly love so well,
It's glory could never be stated
Enough for this person to tell.

Oh Lord, I thank you so
For all these wonderful gifts,
When in spirit I'm feeling low
My heart, in chest, they lift.

Laura Carlisle

OUR BEAUTIFUL WORLD

Our world is full of beauty,
In everything you see,
Let your eyes just feast upon,
Great Mountains and the sea,
Soft petals on the roses,
The blossoms on the trees,
For us, God made this beauty,
He wanted just to please,
Our hearts, with sweet contentment,
Our breaths to take away,
For when you see a sunset,
Your eyes from it, won't stray,
Just also think of snowflakes,
A blanket on the ground,
White hills and trees and fields afar,
Just stand and look around,
It is just like a fairy tale,
With all its magic splendour,
So say a little thank you to,
The one, who is the sender.

Janette Campbell

LITTLE THINGS MEAN A LOT

It's freezing cold outside today.
I think I'll make a cake,
To cheer up all the little ones.
It won't take long to make.

Mix four ounces of breadcrumbs
With a little bit of fat.
Add nuts and cheese, fruit and seeds,
They're sure to love all that.

Press it into little moulds,
Then place in fridge to harden.
An hour later they are done,
So take them down the garden.

Use some string to hang them up,
Onto the washing line.
It's fun to feed God's little birds.
They are all good friends of mine.

Wendy Preece

SIMPLE PLEASURES OF COUNTRYSIDE

Behold, charm of woodland, forest, lea
God's bounteous gifts to all
Cherish, uphold, the plea
This beauty for all to see.

Walk along a country lane,
Such joy to stop, stare
Nature's beauty as on canvas painted
Perfume sweet wafted on scented air.

Flowers shyly peep in hedgerows green
Water trickles into brook near by
Grasses tremble grasshoppers dance unseen
Gentle breezes, berries, leaves, softly sigh.

Honeysuckle on leafy bough entwined,
Blushing foxgloves sway with stately pride.
Song of birds high in sky,
It's peace, solace to soul, the mind.

Lean upon farmyard gate
Pastures green, distant hills to view
God's gifts to enjoy on life's way
Faith hope refreshed with zest anew.

Ivy Lott

THE CLOUGH

One of the most peaceful places on earth
Sits back in the colourful Yorkshire Hills
The unique river flows down the valley
So peaceful the atmosphere thrills.

Deep in my heart my soul and mind
Is where that picture lies
Another like this would be hard to find
Saddened to have to say my goodbyes.

So fresh, the smells of spring,
Still they linger on
Amongst the silver birch and the willow trees
I sang my favourite song.

To the sound of the birds
And the gentle flowing streams
Amongst the poppies I fell asleep in the sun
With all around me I shared my dreams.

So to thank the lord above
For granting me a memory such as this
To of had experienced natural beauty
In the Yorkshire hills
Sheer Bliss.

John Paul Heffernan

SALAD DAYS

the softest summer
gentle grasses sway
in easy breeze
me in my dress
dreaming in the sun
mmm . . .

this warmth
brings us all
a little closer
we open windows
open arms
stand barefoot
touched by magic
this is something good.

R L Knell

THE BEAUTY OF A RAINBOW

Red   - Is the life-blood,
            that flows through us all.
Orange - The rich colour
            Of autumn fall.
Yellow - The sun,
            When it shines through,
            Bathing the world,
            With its amber hue.
Green   - Are the plants,
            and the leaves on the trees.
Blue   - Is the sky,
            and the oceans and seas.
Indigo   - The darkness of night,
            before dawn's golden flame.
Violet   - A tiny flower,
            of that name.

God's glorious gift of colour
Sent to span this planet's girth,
A reflection up in heaven,
Of our beautiful earth.

Brenda Wilding

SPRING

As the mist lifts from the grazing meadow,
And dead leaves dance like wingless fairies in the shadow
Of trees, whose sinewy branches show signs of life,
We rest a moment from toil and strife.
Woods carpeted with bluebells seen;
The wind's now gentle - not so keen.
Birds are busy in their quest
To find materials for a nest.
Bleating lambs with insatiable tums
Stay closely to their mums.
Nature's beauty has no disguise
As viewed through the soul, not the eyes.
To reflect; what is this magic season
That gives us one and all a reason
To often conquer deep despair?
It's Spring; love and hope is in the air.

Maggie Grierson

EVOLUTION CHANGES

Sitting up high in the mountains
Watching the world go by
Streams, rivers and man-made fountains
The sight tells no lie
Who said there was no God?
Who created this before me?
The earth you trod,
The skies to be,
The morning sun
Coming home with the light.
Swiftly the clouds run
Bringing with them the night.
Tell me, in your dream
Did you really see the supreme?

Dex

GOODBYE GREY

Why do raindrops hang on windows, motionless?
Why do grey clouds seem to blow by more slowly then the fluffy ones?
Why do trees stand limp, in saturated monotony?
If rain is clear, why do I see raindrops on my window reflecting gloom and
distance?

Look, close.
Focus on that one raindrop, right there.
Can't you see the glint?

Yes, sort of sparkly and shiny.
What is it?
Colours fly round my room,
Wings of life soar
But what is it?

The grey grows less grey
As a light bursts through
A powerful wind moves, blows back the grey to blue.
See the glint, the sparkle the shining, the colours, the life.

Out of the grey explodes the power
Crimson blood flows revealing its form
Indescribable beauty, awesome glory!
Wow! My Lord *the* artist.

But what of my raindrops?
They roll down my window
They roll down my cheeks,
Out of my heart,
Cleansing a smile.

Here comes the blue, goodbye grey.

Andrew Wolfe

CLOUDS

Clouds in the sky and on the horizon
Are wonders and visions sublime,
Patterns and pictures surprising
Made since the birth of time.

None can dispute the white fluffy cloud
Afloat in a sky of bright blue
Promises summery days,
There is beauty there to view.

Majestic clouds above
Like mountains, towering, bold
Or wrapped like a blanket around
The horizon to gently enfold.

Even grey stormy clouds
Are wondrous to behold
Gathering in strength and form
Lowering, lowering rolled.

Then, as the sun breaks through
The dark clouds lift for sure
And the beautiful scenery of clouds
Is there in the sky once more.

For two clouds are never the same
Or a picture made yet again,
By this panorama of clouds
Controlled by wind, sun and rain.

I find so much beauty there
As I study them high up above,
For they fascinate me so
And clouds I shall always love.

Joan Heybourn

A SUMMER EVENING

Walking along the river bank I decided to have a rest,
To sit and enjoy the English summer at its very best.
Bumble bees buzzing their way from flower to flower,
The ringed bull walking to the hedge, pausing to glower.

A dragonfly hovering above the water, by the reeds,
Waterhen fussing, her chicks following as she leads.
Stately swans, with their arched necks, cygnets ever near,
A lark overhead, its beautiful song is for everyone to hear.

The faint splash of water as the kingfishers dive,
You can hear the quacking as a family of ducks arrive.
Silent the heron as it stands on one leg and waits,
A bullfrog croaks loudly as its throat inflates.

Weeping willow trail in the water as the river flows by
Swallows, swooping and diving, catching insects as they fly.
Disturbed rooks rise above the copse, fly around and protest,
Majestic elms by the roadside, chestnut trees at their best.

In summer, nothing so beautiful as the English countryside,
Green pastures, flowers, tall trees, the vista far and wide.
The air is scented, the horizon fading, far away out of sight,
Shadows lengthen, the English scenery is engulfed in the night.

Frederick Hirst

REFLECTION UPON A ROSE

Profusion of petals
imploding to
infinity

Perfection so modest
that   it   blushes
deep crimson

Lisa Cornwell

9

MY SKY - YOUR SKY - OUR SKY

As I look all around, I see
The beauty in everything you made.
The hills, the sky
The birds that fly
Did you really make it, just for me
The hills, large and green
Are there for all the world to see
You even made them large and white
So they could be seen at night
Did you really make them, just for me
The sky is black, the sky is white,
Even blue when the sun shines bright
In the evenings when you love us so
You make the sky all aglow
Pink-yellow and red
When it's gone it's time for bed.
Did you really make it, just for me
Then, in the morning when I rise
There to greet me, is the sky
The sky you made.
Did you really make it just for me.
The world you made, you made for
All of us!

Lynda Banks

GOD'S WONDERFUL WORLD

How can people doubt you made this world, Lord,
When all around them, miracles are seen?
The colours of the rainbow after rain, Lord,
Show forth Your wondrous handiwork, supreme.

The power of a sudden flash of lightning,
The wonder of the thunder's might, unfurled;
The beauty of a nightingale's song, Lord,
Are proof that You exist, still, in the world.

10

The grandeur of the mountain crowned with snow, Lord,
The splendour of a waterfall's cascade -
Oh! Why do people doubt there is a God, Lord,
When on this earth Your wonders are displayed?

Surveying them, how can they doubt Your presence?
Your wonders in this world are proof, to me;
Please give me, now, the words to move their hearts, Lord,
Inspiring me to win some souls for Thee.

Gail Shepherd

SUMMER

I love the sunlight in summer,
Sunlight at best over summer fields,
Or diffused, filtering down through branches,
In the coolness of the woods.

This was the walk we took,
In July of that hot summer,
Grecian sandals adequate footwear,
No thought of rain in T-shirts and shorts.

Sitting on cold logs, scuffling up the dust,
Picturing encampments of an idealised childhood,
We never had,
Climbing trees, and drinking from streams.

The winter must come soon,
And the memory of this jaunt,
Will seem fantastic, the dryness impossible,
The heat unimaginable.

Wrapped up as we'll be in sweaters,
Shivering, and bad tempered, and wet,
Wondering if it ever happened,
Or will ever happen again.

Susan Thompson

11

WHERE HE IS NEAR

In the midst of noise, this quiet place, is peace . . .
Where mind can tarry . . .
And tethered thoughts, release.
In summer's heat and chase it still knows calm,
A hallowed square of sky
And sleeping charm.
And when feet pass through here
They slow . . . just slightly, for a while
And sometimes hurriers stop to talk, and smile.
Hot brows chill
With some brief and gentle breeze
Wrought by the churchyard's
Ancient Praying Trees.

And lovers pause . . . to kiss
Entwine their hands,
And dream of lace and golden wedding bands.
Like time turned back
No traffic enters here,
Nor any sound to break unkindly in
On those who shed a tear.
And children run around its ring
More quietly somehow, and laughter's stain . . . is soft,
When the Tower Tree whispers in his name,
And eyes turn sleepily aloft.

Kris Dickson

TIME'S UNTIRING FRIEND

In the midst of the forest something seeks for light,
Just a little spark of hope to end the eternal night
A whispering voice within is time's untiring friend,
Who guides travellers to the truth as their journey nears its end,
But the spirit of the shadows will not reveal his face,
For he rules the kingdom of the dark, it is his sacred place.

A multicoloured rainbow displays its wondrous beauty so high above the earth,
For night has been destroyed by the sun's most glorious birth,
The forest fiend has passed away and left his crown behind,
To sit upon the golden sun who gives sight to the blind,
And now the travellers have a friend to guide them on their way,
As they journey merrily through the mist to see a bright new day.

Maurice Caldwell

SUMMER TIME

Feel the soft touch of the summer breeze,
Hear the whisper as it rustles the leaves.
See its ripple on the lush green grass,
On warm summer days that last and last.

Smell the delicate scent of the honeysuckle tree,
Listen to the song of the birds you cannot see.
Rest your tired eyes on nature's colours,
They are there on all the flowers.

Drink the water of the spring so clear,
Eat the fruits from the hedgerows near.
Watch the lark in the sky so high,
See the dragonfly as it flits by.

Across the valley in the green fields,
The fox teaches its cubs age old skills.
Young rabbits near the hedge starts to play,
For now it is nearly the end of day.

Deep in the woods a nightingale sings,
The lovely clear notes of its song do ring.
This long warm summer's day will soon end,
But in a very short time, will start again.

P B Ford

AND GOD SAW THAT IT WAS GOOD

It can be hard in this world
To see beyond the pain,
But if you look through God's eyes
To your heart He will explain,
Remember what Lord Jesus said
That Solomon in all his splendour,
Was never clothed as the wild flowers
So beautiful - so tender,
This world came into being
Of the Father's holy thought
A place born in heaven
Of nature let us be taught,
The sun rises to warm us
The rain waters and feeds,
Earth alive in abundance
Giving life to tiny seeds,
Where do we go to rest?
In the quiet of a sunny glade
By a stream or a mountain path,
We are refreshed by all God made,
Into this comes harmony
For of God we are also from,
When we connect to our Father
Of creation we are one,
As we travel life's journey
May we never lose sight of the view,
Of this splendid - beautiful world
God has given to me and you.

T A Hall

WE MUST TAKE CARE OF THIS WORLD

The sound of a distant tractor
Breaks my reverie
For a while I'd joined those birds on high,
As they flew from tree to tree,
As they wheeled and soared in their joyous flight,
They carried my heart along,
I believe they know of their creator,
And sing his praises in their song.

The plough churns and turns the dark rich soil
In furrows long and deep
In readiness to receive the seed,
For the coming springs early wheat,
Or maybe some other type of crop,
Potato, rape, or swedes
Will send roots searching that fertile ground
For the water it so badly needs.

For this is the way the Lord planned things
With care, with love, with grace
With man, animals, birds and fish
All life must have its place
And the sun, the rain, the wind, the snow
As the seasons chart unfurled
And we the children of our Lord
Must take care of his world.

Don Woods

NATURE

I love to look at nature
The way God intended it to be
Birds and animals living free
Grass and trees a wonderful green
Sit by the sea and watch the waves
Rolling, banging, and cracking in
There you can sit for hours
And after a while you feel good within,
You walk in the woods and there you see,
A deer peeping at you
A woodpecker tapping away so hard,
But he has his beady eye on you,
You'll see old foxy on the prowl
She has her cubs to feed
The rabbit she's been eyeing up
Has gone to ground when she gets near
Nature like life is very hard
But that's what God intended
Yet people kill and ruin these things
Until there lives are ended

Lottie Bugler

THE LORD OF CREATION

See the mountains that reach to the sky,
They were created by the Lord on high,
See the little flowers and the trees so tall,
They were made by the Lord of all.

Well the Lord who created all things,
The lions that roar and butterflies' wings,
The rippling stream and the restless mighty sea,
He's the one who made you and me.

Pauline Wilkins

MY JESUS, I LOVE THEE

My Jesus, I want You to just have Your way,
Whatever You would that I be, do or say;
O help me, my Saviour, to yield unto Thee,
And grant that in all things Thy will I may see.

I want to be like Thee, my Saviour so dear,
I want just to feel Thee for ever so near,
That all that I do, Lord, and all that I say,
Shall be to Thy glory, O help me today.

I want, Lord, to tell someone else of Thy love,
To tell them of that blessed bright home above;
O give me, my Saviour, the grace that I need,
That I may show Jesus in word and in deed.

O grant, Lord, that I may live so near to Thee,
That others around me my Jesus shall see;
O help me to shine in this dark world below,
That many may long my Redeemer to know.

I am longing, my Jesus, Thy dear face to see,
O help me to bring precious souls unto Thee;
That they too may know Thee, be like Thee and reign
With Thee, Lord, for ever, the Lamb that was slain.

Audrey Tuttle

GOD MADE EVERYTHING

God made the colours in the rainbow,
God put the cold in the snowflakes,
He made the Earth and Mars,
God made the hyena's laugh,
God made everything,
He made the moon and stars.

Charlotte Lawrence (6)

GOD HAS

God has a wonderful world
I enjoy it as I see his love unfurl
He created it in six days
We ought to look after it in many ways.
We have a lovely treasure
That I cannot measure,
The earth, the sea, the sky,
We should look after it you and I.

M J Cocks

WHEN YOU'RE NOT HAPPY WITH YOUR LOT

When you're not happy with your lot,
Just stop and think what you have got,
Your health, your strength, your ability to smile,
To walk, to run, or sit a while.

Your sight to see is a wondrous thing,
To see flowers, trees and birds on the wing.
Ears to hear children sing,
Arms to hold and love they bring.

Legs to walk through fields of green,
Where buttercups and daisies can be seen.
Hands to help and show we care,
For those less fortunate in the world out there.

Hearts full of love for everyone,
Minds to think about what's to be done.
So if time you'd take to look around,
There are so many good things to be found.

The next time you moan about your lot,
Just *Stop,* and *Think*, what you *Have* got.

Pauline Patey

MY GARDEN OF MEMORIES

I have a garden, a garden of love
The sun shines on it from Heaven above
A garden of memories, a garden of care
A garden of beauty, it shows everywhere.

A rose bush blooms brightly, a tulip stands tall
Honeysuckle and Ivy climb up the side wall
Lupins sway gently, their flower upright
Reaching for the sky to make the most of the light.

My garden of love, holds memories so sweet
Its glory watched over from the garden seat
A garden of beauty, a garden of grace
My garden of memories, a wonderful place.

Linda Robertson

PEACE OF MIND

Into the forest, I often go to be
Alone with the calmness
Of the falling leaves.

With my mind at rest
I forgot the stress
Then back into the city
With the loud noise and distress.

As I carry on working
To do my best
But the forest is the place
I love the best.

Mark O'Donnell

SEASONS' PRAISE

Song of autumn, hymn of praise,
Season's sadness, sunlit days,
Leaves now turning tawny shade,
Landscape mellow, harvest laid.

Sparkling dawn on silver web,
Drops of dew on silken thread,
Golden cornfield, azure skies,
Purple hills above all rise.

Billowing clouds, whispering breeze,
Wind caressing rustling trees,
Ripening fruit stains the ground,
Sheaves are gathered, fields are ploughed.

Glowing sunset, star-strewn sky,
Pale moon rising shines on high,
Thoughts subdued in autumn haze,
Friendships past and bygone days.

Gentle slumber o'er the earth,
Hush of winter, then rebirth,
Petals falling, soft like rain,
Earth is dying till spring again.

Betty Mealand

I WATCHED A GOLD SUN COMING UP

I watched a gold sun coming up,
A pale moon going down,
A lattice-work of vapour
Softly trellising the town.
And far beyond that windowed sky,
Thrown open to the dawn,
The morning star shone bright with joy
To see a new day born.

Star of love, in love created
By the One who knows
How the faintest gleam of hope
To constant radiance grows,
Point us higher yet to Jesus,
Daystar of our night,
Promise of a certain dawn,
Clear surety of light.

Pat Wray

LITTLE BIRD

Little bird on a branch
feathers fluffed by a breeze;
tips his head, casts a glance;
what was that his one eye sees?

Beetle, bug or earthy worm,
in a flash down he flies;
his prey gone, hop and turn,
another meal he espies.

Filled for now, he joins the wind
carried to another tree . . .
little bird on a branch
what was that his one eye sees?

Large it looms, fur well groomed;
eyes that gleam, glaring;
still as stone, so alone
little bird sits staring.

All at once, in a blink,
leaves and branch are shaken;
little bird, without a sound,
the creeping cat has taken!

Deborah Angell

THE SEAGULL

I saw a seagull swiftly surging
Upwards from the shore,
With slender, stretching neck aloft
It soon began to soar.

With graceful glides it dipped and dropped
On sun-washed, foam tipped waves,
Calling wildly with delight
Above some sailors' graves.

The summer sky then clouded o'er
And pearly drops soon fell;
The seagull moved in panic-flight,
The sea began to swell.

A lightning's streak was followed close
By thunderous tones around,
And heavier rain began to beat
Upon the rock-strewn ground.

The seagull then a shelter sought
To view the darkening scene,
On mossy ledge, in hollow cleft
All damp, so cold and green.

And then the bird was nestled safe
Upon a rocky shelf,
Resting gently on the crag
With seagulls like itself.

Yvonne Watkin-Rees

THANK YOU GOD

Thank you God for nature
For the things of every form,
For the birds that sing each morning
The calm before the storm.
For the sweet smell of the flowers
That bloom along the way,
The busy bees that hurry
Collecting through the day.

Thank you for the trees
They show what life is worth,
They branch out in their beauty
To purify the earth.
The rivers that run endlessly
To join the raging sea,
Without these things around us
Who knows what life would be.

Thank you for the endless dreams
That reach us in the night,
The sun that warms us through the day
The moon that shines so bright.
Thank you for creation
Made for us with love,
Thank you God for everything
You made it all for us.

June Smith

THE BUTTERFLY

Today, I was kissed by a butterfly!
As I sat watching them on my buddleia bush,
Sipping nectar and making love,
I exclaimed at their beauty
And their delicate flight,
        (So soft they flew!)

And as I gazed upon these messengers of God
I felt a light touch on my forehead
Like an angel's kiss:
So quick, so quiet:
In a second, it was gone; then
I turned my face to heaven
And thanked God
For his loving touch on me.

Kathleen Krejci

THE WORLD THAT GOD MADE

This is the world that God made.
This is the sun that shines on the world that God made.
This is the rain that follows the sun that shines on the world that God made,
This is the grass that drinks in the rain that follows the sun that shines
                                on the world that God made.
This is the cow that eats the grass that drinks in the rain that follows the
sun that shines on the world that God made.
We are those who drink the milk given by the cow that eats the grass
that drinks in the rain that follows the sun that shines on the world that
                                God made.
Thank you, God, for the sun and rain and grass and cows and milk,
each part of the world that God made.

Avril Tucker

CREATION

What is all this silly chatter
about a growing lump of matter
have you ever heard such drivel
man grew from a lump of gristle.
Look around you and survey
the live and growing things today,
the wonder of each flying swallow
round the world the sun to follow
animal instinct for survival
in a world of great reprisal.
Each year a tiny seed is sown
into a great big tree is grown
the beauty of each kind of flower
made to adorn a lady's bower.
How can you say that such perfection
is not worked out with clear perception
by the one and only master mind
who guides and helps us who are blind.

K D Smith

SMILES

If I have given you delight,
by anything I have said or done.
Let me be remembered bright,
for the laughter I have spun.

Now for the little thoughts and memory,
that you have borne in mind.
Seek not to question what I be,
but remember just the joy,
that friendship doth us bind.

Alan Noble

HIS NAME

He made the sky a heavenly blue, He made the grass so green,
He gave us the flowers of every hue and eyes for it all to be seen.
He gave us the sun to warm us, the moon to lighten the dark,
He gave us the seats to sit on in this wonderful peaceful park.
He gave us the birds to lighten our worlds, the lambs to gladden our hearts,
He gave us the knowledge to treasure it all, in this world that sets us apart.
From all of the things He created, from all of His works of art,
Until He knows we are sated, and then we are ready to start,
To do all the things He wants us to do, to work for the good of this world,
To bring all His love and happiness too, to each heart and mind and soul.
And when we have done and rest for a while in the wonderful light
        of His love,
We will know that the things that make up our file have been marked by
        Him up above.
Then the sky that we see and the sweet meadow grass, the birds that
        sing in the tree,
All the flowers so bright, in whose perfume we bask, and eyes that
        at last really see,
Were given to us by our Father, who loves all His children the same,
All these things could be made by no other, *Our Father God* is His name.

Winifred Jenkins

THE RAINBOW

The rainbow is a beautiful sight
Especially at first when it's very bright
Seven colours make an arc in the sky
It doesn't last long, alas it will fade and die
It comes in sunshine after rain
It's God's promise he won't flood us again.

Shirley Travis

THE HAND OF GOD

See the sun rise in the morning sky
Bringing light upon the earth anew
See the sun set in the evening time
When at last another day is through
See the beauty of the countryside
Feel the gentle falling rain
Look at all things that are wonderful
And you see the hand of God.

See the trees and flowers in the fields
And the fish within the deep blue sea
See the animals both large and small
Each created individually.
See the changes that the seasons bring
Summer sun and winter snow
Look at all things that are wonderful
And you see the hand of God.

See the stars assembled out in space
High above us in the milky way
See the wonder of the universe
Filled with galaxies in great array
See the moon and its enchanted glow
Sitting there up in the sky
Look at all things that are wonderful
And you see the hand of God.

See the cross on which Lord Jesus died
And the blood he shed upon that tree
See the tomb in which his body lay
Empty now for all eternity
See the risen Lord at God's right hand
There in heaven for us to plea
Look at all things that are wonderful
And you see the hand of God.

H Eley

THE OAK TREE

Trees stand tall and strong, upon the mountain slopes,
Tall pines, their needles, sharp and long.
The winter wind blows through their branches,
Crying in the night.

The plaintive song reaches my ears,
As I stand alone in sorrow,
Dreaming sad dreams,
And thinking of tomorrow.

The cry of the wind speaks to me, calling to my pain,
The pine trees watch in silent rows,
They too know my dream.

To the valley I look,
And see down there,
The mighty oak a quiver,
Lightning strikes,
The tree shines out,
Illumined by the fire.

Its branches twisted and broken,
Yet it lives and grows,
Its strength is never bettered,
Or so it seems to me.

Try to be like that great oak tree,
Weathering the storm,
Growing tall and straight and true,
As your trials you go through,
'Til you reach the haven.

Peter G Thompson

THE WONDERS OF THE WORLD

As I sit in my garden and look at the world
I'm almost convinced God is a girl
To create such beauty that surrounds us all
Moles so tiny and trees so very tall
All the beautiful flowers around my feet
It's an awesome sight gives the eye a treat
I'm sure He didn't think this would go on forever
We take it all for granted, but still take the pleasure
You don't have to move from your own back yard
Watch the birds play but the cats are barred.
A walk in the country see a new furrowed field
Visit again soon and see what it yields
New life emerges all around plant life, wildlife,
From a seed long ago, God had sewn
Sometimes if you look into the sky
It's amazing watching the clouds roll by
Visiting places with mountains so high
And deep deep valleys, just stand and sigh
Seven Wonders of the world, no quite a lot more
Far too many to count hundreds or more by the score
You can travel God's earth and wherever you go
The trees in the meadow the rivers that flow
The wonders of space and the sky at night
Stars all twinkling what a wonderful sight
God created all these for our delight
Many an hour I sit and think, do we,
Really deserve all that the eye can see
It's a wonderful world with quite a few flaws
But no-one's perfect nineteen out of twenty His score
So I'll sit in my garden and *wander* a little more

Sandra Witt

NOURISHMENT FOR POETS' INSPIRATION

This garden of beauty and wonder
Home of the butterflies and bees,
God's art in true revelation
Life abounding give praise from the trees.

This painting of Eden or Heaven
Brush strokes of movement and change,
Artistry in bright living colour
God's creation in orderly arrange.

My garden of refuge and shelter
Home of the fledglings that sing,
Nourishment for poets' inspiration
And sanctuary for fledglings in spring.

Most welcome is spring and summer
After winter dispersion and gloom,
Handicraft of God now apparent
And praise time of nature in bloom.

My garden of retreat and fragrance
No words full justice can give,
God's fountain of love overflowing
On this wonderful world where we live.

Peter James O'Rourke

SO DOTH THE DRAGON-FLY . . .

As a dragon-fly o'er the still waters hovers,
So doth my soul o'er the depths of God;
And as, in the sunlight, iridescent, its wings
Tremble the waters with its colourings,
So doth my soul's longings' pulse
The depths of God most tenderly convulse.

And as from those depths my soul finds succour,
So doth the dragon-fly sun-drench drink;
And as, with God, her longings at one,
My soul riseth, bright, with his Son,
So doth the dragon-fly dart with delight
On its wings, gossamered, 'gainst the night . . .

R John Austin

FORGOTTEN BEAUTY

The things that are so beautiful,
Are things you have forgotten;
Can you recall, the beauty of
The sunrise?
As the beauty of the dawn, gives
Way to early morn.

Did you see the *morning riders*,
As through the woods, they came
A-riding, as the summer day was born.

Did you see, the *jogging cart,*
With the chestnut pony trotting;

Did you hear the pigeon *cooing*,
Did you see the *jackdaws* wooing,
See the bursting rosebud petal,
Like a fluttering angel's wing.

Did you see the royal plumage
Of the *starling* and the *song-thrush*
Did you listen to their music,
Listen to the love-songs, that
Only they can sing.

George Ponting

DAWN

In the east a widening light was paling
the moon's silvery beams upon the waters of the lake,
And tall trees stood like sentinels around the water's edge
whispering the promise of this new day.
Black shadows lightening to a dusky grey
still hiding in their midst the home-going creatures of the night.
Grey mists swirled above the water's surface
turning rosy with the fast approaching light.
The hushed and silent world was waiting
for the signal voices to dispel the night.
Then it came, one lone voice sweetly rising
calling out dispelling night-time's hold.
This golden voice became a chorus, as others
rose to greet the rising sun,
And in the east the widening light turned golden,
Another dawn, another day begun.

Pauline Stocks

LIVING

Why a living brings such sadness,
Sheer brilliance only brings on mere madness.
Is it all that we should know,
So blind we are, to Thee, O' Lord?
Show only us how we should be,
Unlock the Door, throw me the Key.
Wretched creatures, without a will
Or ranting, raving Genius still.
Through the Door, man's only craving,
To see the Light, to stop this wailing.

Patricia Thompson

HARMONY

The sea was deep blue and paler the sky,
A gentle breeze caressed the scene;
The dull gold sand was so soft and so warm,
A moment when all was serene.

I stood quite still on the grassy cliff top
And breathed in the sea-laden air;
Far from my home town's dull polluted skies,
Never breathing too deeply there.

Bees cruised on weather-worn grass at my feet,
Their search for pollen never done,
Seagulls rose sharply with strong steady beat,
Wing flashing pure white in the sun.

It's just the place for a boy and his dad
To play hide and seek on the shore,
As together they peer in clear rock pools
Small crabs and live shells to explore.

The ebb of the tide seems to wash away
The fragile bonds of finite age;
Child discovers, man remembers,
Time softly turns another page.

The joy of living in God's world
Brought a glimpse of heaven to me,
My heart sang with the swirling gulls
Caught in eternal harmony.

Mary Care

THE SWAN

A pale ghost
from out the mist,
has spread its
white cape wide,
and stretched its
long neck to the sun,
as upon the water
it glides.

Its beauty
and its majesty
are reflected
in the lake.
No ripples
and no sound
are heard
as its gown
it shakes.

A silent dancer
dancing
as upon
mirrored gold.
A creature
forever
enchanted,
as if
from stories
of old.

Maria Arnott

THE BEAUTY OF THIS WORLD

One day I sat in the park
And thought about all the beautiful things created by *God*
The birds whistling their tune
They flew from tree to tree
The park so beautiful with roses and ferns and things
Green were the leaves of the trees
Some have flowers, some have doves
I know this earth is a beautiful place
Just look at the skies and a warm glow will take hold of you
Take a trip in a plane
You will see *God's* wonderful works again
If man would only leave the atmosphere
And let us get fresh air again
It would be nice to see people living in harmony
With the *Lord's* handiworks all around us

Just look at the grass, it is so green
Then you keep thinking in Paradise you would be queen
So come along with me to the park
And let's look at *God's* heavenly earth

Thelma Daniels

FOUR WEEKS OLD

I cup my hands to receive it,
So small I can hardly believe it,
Black and round and weighty for its size,
With tiny whiskers and two bright eyes.
New miracle of life, it crawls, not stands,
Yet pressure is felt on the palms of the hands
From four little limbs with proportionate paws
Whose muscles are working to natural laws.
It moves itself round to stare like an owl,
Then voices its thoughts by producing a growl.

Mavis Tulett

THE ARTIST

The artist with his palette, looked down upon the earth,
He then took up his brush, to colour it with verve.
He painted green upon the land, then He called it grass,
He thought of green and brown, painted trees and plants en masse,

He used varied shades and hues, to give each plant distinction,
He painted on fruits with seeds, to save them from extinction,
He became the first gardener, His plants he had to feed,
He gave them rain and sunshine, catering for their every need,

Once again He lifted his brush, using every colour He could,
He painted birds and butterflies, knowing for what reason He should,
Along with other insects, on the ground and in the air,
They were needed to pollinate, their future was in His care.

He painted blue upon the land, rivers, lakes and streams,
Larger blobs were the oceans, He was fulfilling all his dreams,
By the time that He had finished, fauna and flora covered the land,
He sat back and surveyed, what He had created with His hand.

For His final touch, he put man into His painting,
With a bite from one of His fruits, would ensure Him of their mating,
The forms of life that He created, from His colours never-ending,
Would carry on forever, His love for all unbending.

Glennis Horne

THE NAKED WOOD

Only the wind, a naked wood, still hush,
just wind blowing through, tree trunks
white and cracked, branches limp, no green leaves.

Once nesting birds a chorus of lost voices
songs no more, their eggs littered on the
wood floor, green carpet now soil dust,
rabbit holes no more.

The blowing wind an empty chorus, the naked wood
can't take any more, animal carcasses lay on
the soil dust floor.

An open sky looking down on the naked wood,
warrens of life now an empty dust, animals' food chain
gone, stream water swallowed by soil dust, scavenges
food no more.

A wood so green and full of life, taken away by
Man's greed in life.

Garrett John

BIRD WATCH

Swooping and diving,
Cunning - conniving,
Corners cut in their quest for food.
'Tis a clever bird, who thus indeed
  With a wary eye locates the seed,
  Or the peanuts hanging from a tree!
Flitting discreetly from branch to twig,
Back and forth, from tree to bough,
  Agile, watchful,
  In mischievous mood.
I stand and watch in silent delight,
My eyes captured firmly by nature's might.
  A sudden movement -
  An uprush of wings -
  An empty space, where no bird sings.
Darting back in one's and two's,
I silently savour this gladly sight . . .
  My heart thus lightened -
  Uplifted and brightened.
A walk in the garden,
  Disperses *sad* blues!

Freda Ringrose

QUEST

We walked many miles,
Crossing fields, and over stiles,
Little bridges spanning brooks,
Trees close by with cawing rooks
In the pleasant springtime.

As far as I knew,
There were very few
Except us three sisters
Speaking in whispers,
Who knew the secret place
Where the *white* violets grew.

Very scarce, and quite rare,
So dainty, and sweetly scented,
Swaying in the sunny air.
Enchanting fragrant flowers
Hiding amid the long grasses.

The bank was very steep
Clustered with yellow primroses,
Down to the bottom we would leap,
In search of the shy ones
Foregoing clumps of blue tones.

Such joy to find them there
Growing, same place year after year,
Pretty white violets.
We pick a few, and more of the blue
Tied together. A gift for mother.

Madge Thomas

THE SKY AT NIGHT

The sky at night, oh what a lovely
sight, without the clouds the joys
in sight.

By day, the darkness gone, it's right
to fill the land with song, the
birds that sing the milkman bring
the bottle to start our day,
not gin.

On days that's good, the sun
in sight, if we're able to
walk upright.

We may go out and spend the
day, without any work or pay,
we have problems mounted many,
isn't it a shame we don't have
a penny.

Never mind, the rain has gone,
the wind is down, the day has
gone without a frown.

The night returns, the stars
are seen, God's given creation,
and where we've been.

Peter Dawson

THOUGHTS OF PORT NA BA

Upon the cliff top, looking out to sea
The view is so beautiful - God-given and free.
No-one around, and nothing to be heard
'Cept the lap of the waves; and the song of a bird.

The beach down below is warm; smooth and pale,
No footprints have trodden yet to spoil it today.
The clear blue water ripples so softly
Like a whisp'ring sigh - as time passes by.

Three rabbits play at the edge of the sand,
Not far from their burrow in case danger's at hand.
Sometimes they're so still, they can hardly be seen,
When suddenly they move; bobbing tails; wild and free.

The seagulls fly out to catch an early fish,
Swooping on fishing boats in hope of a free dish.
But - 'tis the sound of the oyster catcher's call
You hear early in the morning - first of all.

Out in the distance - Isles Rhum, Eigg and Muck,
In splendour they rise from the depths of the sea
Into the mists of the bright early morn,
A truly magnificent sight to see.

Time seems to stand still in this wonderful place
As I drink in its beauty - its nectar - its grace.
I wish I could stay, watch each season unfurl,
Along with my thoughts - and at peace with the world.

Denise Earnshaw

SALVATION - THE LORD IS MY REFUGE

Cycling along a country lane
Rounding a sudden curve,
Surprised, a partridge hastily
Summoned her scattered brood.
The chicks obeyed the danger call,
Spreading her wings she enclosed them all.

I meant no harm; could not explain
By language, to assure that hen,
Bravely she sat, exposed was she,
A target for an enemy:
Her precious chicks she hid, in fear,
They shelter found: their mother near.

God's wings, so reads His blessed word,
Give full protection, praise the Lord:

He sees my danger, and will spread
Himself, a covering for my head:
Exposed, upon a cross, so high
To save *me*, did My Saviour, die.

His truth, my shield, my buckler, strong,
Lest dashed my foot against a stone;
Safely He guards, by night by day,
My habitation: close I stay,
His wings, my banner, spread above,
Do bear His ensign, see, 'tis *Love*.

'I will say of the Lord, He is my refuge,
My fortress, my God: in Him will I trust.'

Psalm 91, 2.

Eileen M Darke

41

IT'S GOD'S CREATION

When I gaze up to the Heavens, Lord,
And see the works of Thy loving hands,
With the moon and stars above me
I become mindful of Your commands.

Such a awe-inspiring sight,
That lights the darkened skies,
Sometimes bolts of flashing lightning,
So bright before our eyes.

Such power emanates from the Heavens,
But from where we do not know,
And we can feel it in our lives Lord,
It is everywhere we go.

You supply the needs for all the birds Lord,
Gave animals instincts oh so keen,
You planned everything I see Lord,
Sea, mountain, desert, and the grass of green

We thank You Lord for all we have,
Our shelter, food and friends,
Praise God for all He means to us,
Until this earthly journey ends . . .

Ian T Redmond

TO BE ALIVE

If we stop and look and listen for a while
At things around us, tarry, and smile
Our heart will be lifted, we will be glad
For all God's bounty that can be had

The blackbird singing out to its mate
The primroses growing dainty by the gate
The leafy trees, rose garden perfume
The promise of what will come soon

The warm rays of the sun on high
The water babbling through the brook
Just stand a while and look
Take it all, in the sights and sounds
That life is with you all around

It will make you glad to be alive
Give you a spur to exist, and survive,
And in the future you can look forward to
Being part of the scene God gave to you
To enjoy

Doreen M Brown

GOD'S WONDERFUL WORLD

Gentle waves beat against the glistening golden sands,
The perfection of a tiny new-born baby's hands.
A crisp dew that falls, on a spider's web just formed,
Glistening sumptuous honey, after the bees have swarmed.
A fresh patch of snowdrops, hidden beneath the snow,
For God's wonderful world, seems to grow and grow.

Stars that sparkle, over a long winding river,
A touch from a lover, that sends the body to a quiver.
The graceful moon, floating above the dark craggy mountains,
Perfect images of tranquillity, cascading from fountains.
Sparkling champagne, poured in a long elegant glass,
For God's wonderful world, shall never be a farce.

Dawn breaking, bursting through the picturesque night,
A fiery ball of flames, is such an incredible sight.
Crocuses opening their petals, basking in the sun's rays,
The colour of the rainbow, on wet rainy days.
I glance at the horizon, a heron flies towards the sun,
For God's wonderful world, is created for everyone.

Martina Quennell

BECAUSE IT'S THERE

During an interview with a mountain climber,
I enquired why he scaled those dizzy heights.
So he took me to the foot of the towering peaks;
Laying down his weighty ropes, he scanned my eyes
And told me - because it's there.

During a discussion with a daring swimmer,
I queried why she swam the cold channel.
So she ferried me back to the shore;
Disposing of her grease and oil, she surveyed my eyes
And declared - because it's there.

During an audience with a brave astronaut,
I was curious as to why he flew to the Moon.
So he escorted me to an unobstructed sacred space;
Transferring the controls of his satellite, he explored my eyes
And stated - because it's there.

During a lecture with the mountain climber,
The swimmer and the astronaut
They took a risk, and looking into my eyes
Questioned my faith and why I went to church;
So I testified - because He's there.

Margaret A Holland

NATURE

The shapes in the garden
The colour, the perfume
All originates its magnificent blooms
Lupins stand splendid, delphiniums too
Poppies, azaleas to name but a few
All God's creations, is infinitely foretold
How wonderful, creative
Magnificent and bold.

Irene Pearce

GOD'S WONDERFUL WORLD

To watch a child and win a smile,
With her a kitten plays the while,
Questing paw on chubby knee -
Did ever man more beauty see?

- Watch butterflies, those winged leaves
Of hues so bright - those flower thieves,
The humming bees, delight the sun
And bless God's work while ages run.

Elizabeth Glover

GOD'S WONDERFUL WORLD

Of all the wonders of God's earth,
So many can I recall, an
opening flower, a bird in full
flight, a robin on a wall, to
feel the warmth of the sunshine;
or the sand between your toes;
to travel to a far and distant
land, where the winding river
flows; you can travel as far
as Egypt, if you saved up
enough fare; or travel the Lochs
of Scotland, if you're lucky, Nessie
may be there, but with so
much in your own home
town you needn't ever stray,
as the wonders of the world are
never very far away.

Susan Caroline Gamble

THE LOVE TOWER

Shadows cast amidst the people,
Looking up and down the steeple,
Some admiring its glorious beauty,
Others carrying out their duty.

Here I stand too,
Watching the tower's dew
Fall among the leaves upon the ground,
And nowhere to be found.

Maybe one day the tower will fall,
Nothing will be there to stand tall,
No dew, no night, no love,
Just the old and haggard dove,
Of paradise!

Ann Marie Wintrip

WHEN LITTLE BIRDS THEIR VOICES RAISE
GOD SMILES AT THEIR SONGS OF PRAISE

(Mattthew 10:29)

One day, when all the prayers are said,
And all grateful voices have been heard;
Remember, that tiny piece of bread?
It made a banquet, for a hungry bird.
He soaring high into the sky,
Sang to *God*, and thus was blessed;
Then, filled with joy did homeward fly,
To feed the mouths within his nest.
When great and small, unto *God* pray,
And offer *Him* their thanks all day,
He pours out *His* love, before we call;
For 'tis He that marks a sparrow's fall.

Les G Moss

46

HIS PRESENCE

We may hear a blackbird sing,
Sing a song of joy,
Or see a skylark on the wing,
They're both in God's employ.
We may hear children laughing,
Laughing as they play,
Or smell the fragrance of a rose,
The breeze has sent our way.
We may see the honey bee,
Or the butterfly,
Gaze up at the sky of blue,
And watch white clouds drift by.
While everything is peaceful,
We relax and smile,
At the subtle way God tells us,
He is with us all the while.
But He is not always subtle,
He can spring a surprise
And can quite drastically
Open up our eyes.
While we're sleeping peacefully,
In our beds at night,
He may well remind us,
Of his power and might,
By a brilliant lightning flash,
And a deafening roar,
As He sends a thunderstorm,
To fill our hearts with awe.

J Preece

CLOUDS OF BEAUTY

Look up at the sky on a summer's day
and the clouds will hold you enthralled.
Their feathery wisps, and cotton wool balls,
gild the heavens in a radiant way.

And sometimes the clouds form shapes
in that glorious blue of the sky.
A lion, an elephant, a tree or a boat,
and some humans in white flowing capes.

In the evening, the dying sun casts
a wonderful prism of colour.
A rainbow without any rain,
that fades when the long day is past.

Then the clouds turn a much darker shade,
and bluish grey tints each one,
and the feathers that brightened the day,
at eventide, wither and fade.

At night, dark purple paints the sky,
and the beautiful day disappears.
A million stars spangle that heavenly vault,
and the planets and moon shine on high.

When dawn breaks, the sun shines again,
and day begets day after day,
for the clouds and the sky will endure
forever, through sun, winds and rain.

Daphne Richards

SHERINGHAM PARK

I love to walk in Sheringham Park,
When the rhododendrons bloom,
A myriad of vibrant colour
So delicately shown.
Azaleas in all their beauty
Fragrance spread around,
And many coloured petals,
Covering the ground.

I hear a robin singing,
And see his coloured breast,
As he sits among the branches
Just above his nest.
A singing thrush, a blue tit,
A blackbird on the ground,
Then way up in a dead tree,
A woodpecker is found.

Along the Rhododendron Drive,
Feeling like a queen,
I soak up such a wondrous sight,
That ever there has been.
A toad hops on the pathway,
A child bends to look,
The picture is more marvellous
Than anybody took.

In awe of God's creation
I drift along my way
How carefully He makes things
Miraculously today.

Linda Smith

DANCING DAFFODILS

Many buds in shades of green
Burst forth on every bough
Plants all through winter sleeping
Awake and peep through now

It seems the world is born anew
Many treasures to behold
Soft clouds of fragrant blossom
Dancing daffodils of gold

Sweet little birds sing out their song
A choir fit for kings
They fly around the garden
So many coloured wings

I am completely hypnotised
By this beauty that I see
How I love my heavenly Father
Who gave all this to me

Spring also does remind me
What Jesus said of me and you
That when our body we must leave
Our spirit lives anew

Angela Pearson

AUSTRIA 1970

Rivers of water, white as snow,
Flowers in bud, warm winds that blow,
Cascading falls, a million trees,
This is the land, the heart doth please.

Rocks by the wayside, chatter of birds
Yodelling natives, speeches, words,
Sunlight on churches, cruel slopes
Nursing the youthful climbers' hopes.

Swift flowing river, avalanche fear,
Picturesque graveyards, often a tear
Light on the mountains, clouds in the skies
Vehicles humming, family ties.

Rest by the wayside, hearts that are faint,
View God's creation, sinner and saint
Leave earthly toil, and converse staid
To the Creator praises be paid.

Peter Buss

BEAUTY OF NATURE

How many times have I seen the moon
High up in the sky
And watched the many different clouds
As they go scudding by.

How many times have I smelt the perfume
Of a lovely garden flower
But soon the petals are falling
In a warm summery shower.

How many times have I heard the wind
Making an eerie sound
Rustling the leaves and moaning
Swirling around and around.

How many times have I felt the sun
Beating on my head
Lying in the long tall grass
A hollow for my bed.

How many times have I heard the birds
Singing their lovely song
The blackbird, the thrush the nightingale
I could listen all day long.

Jeanette L Durk

GOD'S WONDERFUL WORLD

I don't know why I want to express in words, what
I see in this wonderful world. It just comes
to me. Didn't the Lord say 'I'm in you and
you're in Me.' If one believes He created it all -
including his flock, then who else is
carrying on His work - in those He chooses, in
different ways. To my mind He is the Power,
the Life, eg the Living Spirit in everything.
He told us so, it's so simple - He looked on
His creation and saw it was good - isn't
that what we're doing too?

To appreciate and see it as He does.
We're just letting Him pass His words on -
In us - or, that's how it seems to me.

Muriel M Owen

FOUR SEASONS' WALK

As I walk down the windy path,
Thro' the woods and up the Garth,
I hear the trees a-rustle,
And the birds a-singing.
And the autumn through the meadows gold,
Picking blackberries,
Or go playing in that yellow hay, I take my dog,
And off she doth bound,
Through summer bracken,
And chase rabbits,
In the winter,
In my horse and cart,
To feed the sheep,
Whose little warm lambs,
Frolic in the snow.

Julia Crake

THE LORD THE ARTIST

When the sun extends September rays,
filtering the woodland ways,
what joy to tread a leafy lane
and smell the cool earth moist with rain.

To marvel at the mystery,
at that which turns the once green trees
to golden brown and russet shade,
warming every leaf and blade.

Then glides around the firethorn mellow
to spray the berries red and yellow,
and fires the old house walls to flame,
crimsoning from soil to frame.

It dyes the hillside richest bronze,
burnishing the bracken fronds,
and clambers up the maple tree,
to tint its leaves mahogany . . .

Hastening on it takes the brush,
to rouge the apple's cheeks to blush
and ripen to maturity,
bending the bow with gluttony.

What joy to feast the eyes on all
these mellow shades before the fall,
before the glowing canvas changes,
and *He* the artist rearranges.

Ivy Wood

THE WONDER OF LIFE

Look around and you will find
Just what God had in mind
When He created this world for us
Without a great deal of fuss

Watch a bird in full flight
Isn't it a beautiful sight?
A butterfly flits gracefully by
Way up in God's blue sky

The green of the grass and the trees
Swaying in a gentle breeze
An ocean so deep and blue
God made for me and you

God's creatures great and small
Can be enjoyed by us all
All these things you see around
Flying high or on the ground

How can you be in doubt
That God's influence is all about
The wonders of God's world can be
Enjoyed each day by you and me.

Jean Bradbury

THE SUNSET

As I was coming down to church,
The sun was bending low,
Across the sky was a sunset bright,
Painted by . . . Michaelangelo?

No. It was painted by my Lord,
Like all that comes from Him,
It was perfect in its colouring
And it made the world look dim.

So as I travelled on to church
I thanked the Lord on high
For giving me a perfect sunset
To gladden my heart and eye.

So thank the Lord for simple things,
Those that happen every day,
And the Lord will bless you mightily
In each and every way.

Ann Brown

SIMPLE PLEASURES

Have you opened your door in the early morn as the sun first kissed the skies
And glistened on the dew-dropped leaves like an ocean of tear-filled eyes
Or heard the birds proclaim the dawn in unison of song
The cattle lowing on the lea - or streams that go gurgling on
Have you breathed the perfume of a rose - from the heavenly
                                                    rain-washed store
Of fragrance from a garden that loving hands adore
Or watched the clouds go scudding by like galleons from the past
The swirling winds in boisterous mood astride their wispy masts
Sat quietly in transient pose as gentle breezes play
A lullaby on the dancing reeds in the moonlight's silvery rays
Or strolled along a sandy shore - with windswept spray-flecked hair
While salt-filled ripples soothe a mind preoccupied with care
P'raps wandered over craggy hills with distant views enchanted
Intoxicated by the scent of heather no-one's planted
Heard the nightingale in leafy lane - full throated in its praise
Of the creator's orchestration of nature's wondrous ways
These are the wonders of the world - amongst its greatest treasures
For once experienced - then you've scaled the heights of simple pleasures
No sculptor's chisel, artist's brush could reproduce for me
The glory in the beauty of nature's panoply.

John Elias

55

DO YOU EVER?

Do you ever wonder why?
Sigh a little sigh,
Cry a little cry.
Do you ever wonder why?
When you're sad, feeling bad.
At a love that cost so dear.
At a love that feels so near.
At a love that runs so deep.
And it's yours and yours to keep.

Marion Cook

DECIDUOUS TREES

Deciduous trees are just like people,
They alter with the passing of time.
Each season they acquire a different dress,
Hoping small birds and animals to impress.
Exactly like young girls in their Sunday best,
They long to look different from the rest.
Trees have a magnificence all of their own,
Far different from other plants I have grown.
Their strength comes from within their torso,
I suspect other plants wish they were strong also.
Leaves act like fingers blowing in the breeze,
But blossoms are the prettiest colours to please.
Evergreen trees do not have the same appeal,
The sheen of their leaves makes them seem not real.
But deciduous trees age like people do,
If they could speak, would they to you?
My favourite trees have all to be admired,
Without them the world would be a duller place.

Susan Mullinger

HEAVEN ON EARTH

At last the long lazy days have begun,
Engulfed by the rays of the warm summer sun.
A gentle breeze plays music through the trees,
The song of the lark, the humming of the bees.

Oh! To lie naked as the day,
Warm winds bathe my body as I lay.
This is the closest I can ever be,
To the wonders of nature that God gave to me.

Flowers in bloom, butterflies galore,
Who could ask for anything more?
I have ears to hear with and eyes to see,
All these wonderful things that were given to me.

Carol Latchford

GENESIS REVISITED

God said
Let there be light
And there was light
And He continued creating the world
In much the same way
Speaking life into being
Out of nothing
And sometime ago
He said
Let there be Claire
And let her have green eyes and freckles
And a love for poetry
And here I am
Honoured to be
A small but integral part
Of God's beautiful creation

Claire Handscombe

SPRING

How rich a blessing just to look
At what our God created -
The fluffy clouds - the changing skies -
It makes me feel elated.

The smell of *freshness* in the air
After a shower of rain.
The growth of pretty flowers
Bursting forth again.

The beauty of creation
Speaks to my joyful heart
And the changing of the seasons
As they come and then depart.

The bulbs beneath the hardened ground
Break forth to greet the Spring -
And talking birds meet once more
As they take flight on wing.

The squirrels play on ground and tree -
And birds provide much chatter.
God providing homes for them -
(To Him it really does matter)

From observing nature
We learn from God above.
'Consider thy heavens' - reflective words
Full of meaning and wonderful love.

Pat Melbourn

WORLD'S GLORY

As I sit looking out to sea
The vast horizon beckons me
I think of all the things out there
Of beauty and culture the world has to share
No one person could ever possess
The grace and glamour or great prowess
The circumference of the world is vast
Many things are made to last
Things that are built or simply grown
No one person should treat as their own
Beautiful things should be shared around
And left to flourish as they're found
I'd love to journey far and wide
To walk with others by my side
The natures of the world are free
Leave them there for all to see
I've never been abroad as yet
So make the most of what I get

Marion Pollitt

MY DESIRE (INSPIRED BY A BIRD)

Lord let me be free like a bird in you,
To fly and soar to places you would take me,
To rise up over daily circumstances that keep me down,
And swoop eagerly to reeds I see around me,
May my daily songs be cheerful ones to you,
And your presence felt by others as I pass by,
Help me raise my young in the ways you have provided,
And protect them under the shadow of your wing,
That they may grow strong with love for you,
And be free like a bird to reach others too.

Diane Mackintosh

THE WORLD AROUND US

The world is such a beautiful place
Its beauty will put a smile on your face
Consider the birds, the flowers, the trees
The honey that's made from the buzzing bees

From one seed that's planted many will grow
How it happens we do not know
It's a wonder that makes me stand in awe
When planted, to produce is a natural law

The stars at night are a wondrous thing
The birds they fly with outstretched wing
The trees they sway in the gentle breeze
I thank my God upon my knees

The sun that shines, the sea, the sand
To walk with your child hand in hand
To have a picnic beside the lake
These beautiful things my God did make

The moon that lights the sky at night
It too was made by the God of might
In this beautiful world His presence I feel
Through it, my God to me is real

And that's the reason I write of this world
I feel God's love to me unfurled
The beauty of nature can change a sad face
For the world we live in's a beautiful place

Janet McBride

MY GARDEN

I miss you so much -
Up here in my flat;
And remember with longing,
Happy days when I sat
Surrounded by roses
      Delphiniums blue;
      Daisies and larkspur,
      Geraniums too.

I watched the red robin,
The sparrow, the finch -
Each in his own place -
They knew every inch!

Blackcurrants, blackberries,
Were there in galore;
Apples, so rosy -
ready to store.

Picnics in summer;
tea on the lawn,
An Englishman's heaven
To greet each new dawn.

Outside - there's a car park
for all the smart cars;
Soon 'twill be a launching pad
to take us to Mars!

Turn back the clock, please -
Don't think me a bore!
In my garden of ease
Just let me linger once more.

Betty Wilson

THESE I LOVE

I love the fragrance of the lilac tree,
As day by day its lovely flowers unfold
The air is sweetened as we fill each room,
And purple blossoms give us joys untold.

The willowy pear tree, gowned in pearly white,
Her bridal branches tossing to the sky,
Virginal beauty, graceful and serene,
And sending glorious perfume up on high.

And when I see a shady bluebell wood
Like a blue carpet, flecked with tints of green,
With sunlight slanting through the tall high trees,
My glad heart lingers with the lovely scene.

But in September, when the days are cool,
My wish to tramp the moors will never cease.
The purple heather sets my heart on fire,
My arms are laden and my soul's at peace.

At evening, when the sun sinks o'er the hills,
And sends a glow across the western sky,
The beauty of that scene comforts my mind,
For now I know that sleep and rest are nigh.

Margaret Turtle

EASTER

With Easter comes our spring time,
We see new life appear,
Trees in bud, the weather fine,
Past are days cold and drear.

Birds give pleasure with their songs,
Baby lambs start bleating,
People come out in their throngs,
Happy Easter greeting.

We emerge from winter's snow
Rejoicing in the spring.
Thanks to God that we can go on,
To hear church bells ring.

Summer, autumn, winter too,
The farmer's seed his sews,
So pray to God all of you
As each year comes and goes.

Suzanne Joy Golding

HARVEST HOME

Through a stained-glass window
The autumn sun breaks through
To shine on fruit and vegetables
And flowers of tawny hue

Shiny, polished apples
Tomatoes, glowing red
Centrally in pride of place
The plaited Harvest bread

Marrows, worthy of a prize
Onions by the score
Chrysanthemums in vases
With eggs arranged on straw

Ripened ears of golden corn
Beneath the pulpit laid
Beside flamboyant dahlias
Artistically displayed

The congregation rise to sing
The well-loved Harvest hymn
Of scattering seed and ploughing
All safely gathered in.

Sheila Leheup

GOD'S WONDERFUL WORLD

This is a lovely world of ours.
Long before the motor cars.
Country lanes we would love to walk,
Chatting away.
We would love to talk.
Watching the birds, building their
nests, flowers growing under
hedgerows rest.
Violets, white and blue.
Primroses, cowslips, buttercups too.
Handfuls picked, home we would go,
          paddling in the brook,
Under the hot summer sun.
Cows in the field, did graze and moo.
Pigs in the sty, did stare at you.
You may see a fox, owl in the tree,
hedgehog asleep rolled up in a ball.
The glory of the world.
I love it all.

Margaret Brown

THIS PLANET BEAUTIFUL

From God's hand . . . the elements;
        of fire air and water,
        abundantly - evident.

Form the Earth . . . a creation;
        autonomously vibrant,
        a living - sensation.

Of life . . . a selection;
        self preservation,
        a cosmic - reflection.

David Surman

64

DAYBREAK

We'll sit in the silence of this room
The start of a brand new day
We'll watch the sunrise in a glorious light
And see the moon just drift away
The stars will now rest
The warmth will come through
The birds will start singing their song
As we sit and ponder
The thoughts will drift in
What will be in store today
We feel Your love and presence so strong
Just a thought we can link up and see
This glorious Light has begun
For all mankind and Thee.
Please teach us Your lesson
We lean on your power
We need to go forward
Just think of the sunrise
And I think I'll be with Thee.

Margaret Edith Craggs

GOD'S GARDEN

There's other times and other places
When you're fed up with those well-known faces
Just wander along that avenue
Of copper clad trees and golden hue.

Just tarry where the robin sings
And bathe in the joy that this sound brings
Let your heart be merry and your mind be light
In God's garden clear and bright.

Mary Hayworth

65

IN ALL ITS GLORY

In the heat of the sun
And the cool of the breeze,
The clouds rolling by
With the wind in the trees.

The waves of the sea
Come crashing in,
Pebbles and shells
Left from within.

Rivers and stream
Running around,
Plant and fishes
Not making a sound.

Cows and sheep
Wheat and corn,
Apples and plums
Misty morn.

Grass so green
Birds up above,
This beautiful country
We really should love.

Marlene M Gilbert

WHEAT AND TARES

That wheat and tares together grow
God's wisdom has elected.
I wonder why this should be so?
Is wheat left unprotected?
We find the struggle hard and long,
The wheat is choked, the tares are strong
And we are oft faint-hearted.

Yes, wheat and tares together grow
Until this life is ended.
But what God's love saw fit to sow
Is by His aid defended.
So we must toil and *use* His grace
'til, battle-scarred, we gain our place,
The tares at last uprooted . . .

Patricia D S Linton

OUR GARDEN

We think we've the best garden in town
When it is quiet, we come out and look around!
In the far secluded corn we've made our nest,
Safe and warm, for our little ones to rest!

Sitting on our carpet of grass so green,
From this position, the whole garden is seen!
With rockeries cascading like a waterfall,
And fur trees, that seem to stand so tall.

Pots bubbling over with a rainbow of plants,
With reflections on the pond doing a dance!
And flowers that open with the raising sun,
Then go back to sleep when the day is done!

Weeds hoping to grab a position to grow,
But when folks spot them, they have to go!
With bushes that are trimmed to shape,
While others are fighting to over take!

There's also an understanding amongst plants,
Why some come and go, to give the others a chance!
So there is an ever changing sea of colour,
Come and have a peep, but don't blow our cover!

Penelope Ann

SOUL GROWTH

There was birdsong in the depot
and my mind had gone away,
so the shrill tweet-tweet of birdish beaks
allowed my soul to stay.

I found water in the desert
and my mouth had dried right up,
but the liquid fuel so clear, so cool
allowed my soul to sup.

There was fire in the ice-box
and my ears were frozen raw,
so the cooling flame, that left no pain
allowed my soul to thaw.

But love itself is hatred -
from one source both are thrown;
By finding this, in a hurtful kiss
My soul has begun to grow!

Terence Stacey

FRUITFULNESS

Life is a walk through desert land
So many footprints in the sand
We need to be full of God's heavenly power
To pour out his spirit, to bring to flower
The ones who feel lost without knowing why.
Their lives so meaningless, empty and dry.
They need our prayers to help them grow
Until out of them, living waters flow
And then at the end we will look back to find
Not a barren desert harsh and unkind.
But a land that is cared for watered and sown.
A garden of glory to be God's own.

C Sheward

THE SOUTH EAST COAST OF ENGLAND

How still the view on such a day!
The cliffs of France are clearly seen,
The boats like cardboard cut-outs are
On molten silk of blue and green.

The sea, it does so solid look,
Seems one could walk across to France.
And when the sun upon it shines,
Liquid diamonds flash and dance.

On looking out towards the West,
One can see the Sussex Downs;
And out of sight beyond the hills
Reside the Southern coastal towns.

But, looking West and farthest South -
A landmark there for all to see -
The buildings for atomic power
Supplies the grid for you and me.

At Dungeness, one also finds
A haven sure - the birds respite -
Where, when arriving from abroad
Rare and common pause from flight.

The South-East point of England here,
With perfect views and fresh sea air
Is where I ever want to be.
No other place is quite so fair.

Margaret M Sherwood

RIVER OF LIFE

Life is like a river, never still
Dependent on its knowledge and its skill.
Starting as a trickle it becomes
Mature, adult, forever on the run.
Serene in the shallows peacefully
Then rushing in the rapids, wild and free.
Full of life, abundant, daring, bold
Destiny the ocean's depth its goal.
Thrashing onwards over rocks and sand
Surging against barriers and dams.
Cascading over mountains fierce and strong,
Lashing in the tempest, spitting foam.
Laughing in the sunshine's gentle beams
Meandering through valleys as in dreams.
Whispering with the breezes soft and warm
Washing over pebbles at first dawn.
Sleeping as it caresses the night
Whilst still awake to greet the new daylight.
Such is life an endless test of skill
Rapids and then aftermath, so still.
Laughing and crying in the sun
Always rushing, never walk, but run
Bubbling with joy, daring bold
From the start of life until the old.
Pebbles come to hamper and forestall
Yet we hurry on to ocean's call
Sleeping yet awake, our senses keen.
Once a trickle onward gurgling stream.
Onwards ever onwards river strong
Searching for the goal where we belong.

Sonia Santina

MY KINGDOM

The gorse upon the heath, the springy grass beneath,
The racing clouds above - these are the things I love.

The falling dry-stone wall, the blackbird's happy call,
The skylark's grassy nest - these things I love the best.

The crimson sun at dawn, the flagstone path, time worn,
The wooden halfway seat where I can rest my feet.

My dear dog's joyous bark, the soaring of the lark,
I never can be poor when I have these, and more.

The slow rise of the hill, Heath village, quaint and still,
Where nature plays to me her silent melody.

The priest's house rests serene atop its chain-fenced green,
The Dower house supplies food for my hungry eyes.

And dominating all, the stone pilastered hall,
The fingers on whose clock man's vain contrivings mock.

Small homes and mansions blend as dreamily I wend
Along enchanted ways where sun with shadow plays.

Trees like a mighty nave, grass windblown like the wave,
The distant church's spire, the western sky afire.

I see the nightfall greet its wildlife, timid, fleet.
These I would not exchange could I the whole world range.

Please God, give me the health to walk among this wealth.
Let money pass me by; we're rich, my dog and I.

Jessie Edwards

DO WE REALLY LIVE IN A WONDERFUL WORLD?

Is it really a pleasure to live in God's wonderful world?
Sunshine and flowers and the sound of music can be heard,
the promise of nice things to come,
a family to take care of me,
in spite of all the world's problems,
I know I am happy.

I see disaster on the news,
pollution, a world of abuse,
vandalism, hatred in my street,
is anyone honest, whom I see?
But inside my house I can close the door,
I know I am safe, I care no more,
God's wonderful world is really a disgrace,
but it's not his fault, it's the human race,
people should change and not look to blame,
innocent people it's always the same,
we can change and start to care
and make God proud that we are there.

God's wonderful world can be wonderful once again,
if we can overcome the abuse and the pain,
we can be friends and reach out our hands across the seas,
to the rest of our world family who live in misery,
we can change and make them agree,
that God's wonderful world can be wonderful for all to see.

Claire Young

PICTURE

The mountains climb up to the sky,
Majestic snow peaks way up high,
And in the valley's shades of green
A village nestles, gentle scene.

An eagle soars as if in joy,
The clouds like child's dreams as they fly,
Some dark, some light, but none to last;
Each floats softly along, then past.

The sky above is blue and deep,
The little houses look asleep.
The church points up, with spire of hope,
And shadows drift across the slope.

The greens and blues and whites and greys
All blend in artistry of praise;
The little birds too, bathe in sounds
The atmosphere; all peace abounds.

People are nowhere to be seen,
But all amidst this joyous scene,
The working, loving, still goes on,
Until the day of life is done.

This 'scape is one of grandeur bright,
Created gentleness and light.
I gaze in awe, and understand
The glory our Creator planned.

Such harmony is here to see;
I want it to be found in me,
That I might one with beauty be,
Here in God's land of Italy!

David Herring

THE DAWN

The break of day!
'Seek and ye shall find'.
Let us look for beauty
To fill the heart and mind.

The break of day!
What's that I hear?
A blackbird's song.
Come, praise and sing along!

The break of day!
What's that I smell?
The honeysuckle flower,
Scent of new-mown hay.

The break of day!
What's that I feel?
The gentle breeze, falling dew.
I feel refreshed!

The break of day!
What's that I see?
A newborn calf,
Lambs at play.
I feel so blest.

The break of day!
Come, kneel and pray,
And thank our Creator
For all the blessings
Along the way.

Mary Herring

POET SHOULD I BE

Throw the net
Into the sea
Let it dance
Amongst the waves
Or
Let it sink
Or snag a rocky cave.
Poet should I be?
Product of the wind
Bearer of fire
Flighty as the air.
I breathe . . . and await
What mystery?

Evelynne Goldberg

THE WONDER OF LIFE

Do you ever wonder why
The moon and stars light up the sky,
Why rainbows shimmer overhead
The rising sun's a brilliant red.
Do you stop to think about
How wet the rain can be,
How vivid is the lightning
That disturbs our reverie.
We take for granted all these things
The wind, the rain and sun,
Accepting seasons come and go,
As God just having fun.
Give a little deeper thought
To the elements we share,
If it wasn't for these miracles
You and I would not be here.

Margaret Malenoir

NORWAY

Standing
In awesome wonder, fear,
Gazing
At the infinite beauty
Of Your creation,
Speaking to me
Of You.

The rich, deep, blue vastness of the fjord,
Silent and full.
Wild, rugged mountains, snow-capped peaks,
Their strong, powerful outlines protruding boldly
Into the cloudless sky.
Vast sweeps of dark green pines,
As far as the eye can see;
Dense, but beautiful.

From the waterfall,
Tumbling silently,
An everlasting flow of beauty, splashing
Down the sheer rock face.
All is protected by the warmth of Your sun,
And the ceaseless melody of Your birds.

Doubts fade;
A still, overwhelming peace is all around me,
Inside me, flooding my being.
The perfection of unspoilt nature
Speaks of the reality of Your power
And truth,
Creator.

Pauline Clark

IMPRESSIONS

Warm-mauve clouds that move north-east
The blazing light that's increased
Silhouettes of chimney pots
Handfuls of forget-me-nots

The damp wind, and a magpie
Black and white, against the sky
Now he's gone, hunting his prey
As the wind blows hard today

Cream-coffee house on the block
Window closed without a lock
Gull dipping, and caught in the wind
Feel pate, where hair has thinned

Clouds become cream and blow fast
Where were my eyes in the past?
A flock of birds goes over
Who'll find a four-leafed clover?

The windy bush flickers and groans
Help me get rid of my moans
The laurel is full of life
Nature isn't void of strife

Candle burning for our pain
That we be made one again
Clear blue skies, and love that's free
Lord please use Your love through me

Madonna with eyes of love
Strength needed in the push and shove
Humble me *Lord* in my pride
Let me know Your love inside

Richard Reddell

SEED TIME AND HARVEST

Patchwork; yes, intricate,
But no random implantation.
No casual delineation.
Apportioned beauty, spreading feast-like
For the soul's replenishment,
The eye's contentment.
Surely the Lord is here; His majesty alone
The imagery's designer - far beyond
The limited confines of our minds.
His ever-changing, allocated seasons
And awesome wonder of his given gift
From God to man shall never fail.
His promises are sacrosanct,
Whilst we, recipients, can contemplate
With praise such love, that trusts
His earth to us.

Anne Smithers

SPRING FLOWERS

The Christmas rose and the snowdrop, the first of spring flowers
They bloom in midwinter amid frost and snow showers
Their perfect beauty on the ground cold and bare
Always amaze me, and I just stand and stare

The jasmine, crocus and daffodils come next
All golden and yellow, as one would expect
Their cheerful colour heralds the spring
With the longer light days, and all that they bring

The Easter festival comes along in the spring
When 'Jesus' died on the cross to save man from sin
So we decorate churches gay with palms and spring flowers
To praise and adore 'Him' this great God of ours.

M A Ivel

GARDEN PEACE

There is peace in your garden,
On a lovely summer's day,
Butterflies give sweet kisses
On your flowers as they sway
It's God's world let it be
The colours of the flowers
Forever there for all to see.
The birds in their joyful flight
So full of love from tree to tree
A little greed as they eat the seed
Yet they live in harmony
Because God will ever be
Their creator of earth sky and sea
Such wonder no man could ever make
Yet some think it's all a fake.
When will they ever wake
To the beautiful and tender love
Of God in heaven from above
His creation is stirred with hate,
By men whose crime will never end
Till they clasp the hand of tender care
Of fellow men in love and prayer,
The bitterness, of the hate
Of evil men who rob and rape
They shield themselves
With the devil's cape
Breaking up this wonderful world
A joy forever but it's all unfurled.

Blanche Naughton

THE LORD'S CALL

Please don't call me in the springtime
For you know I love to hear
The singing of the birds and
The cuckoo loud and clear

Please don't call me in the summer
For you know I love to see
The lovely flowers growing
And hear the humming of the bee

Please don't call me in the autumn
For you know I love to see
The leaves of orange, red and gold
Upon a sleepy tree

Please don't call me in the winter
For you know I love to see
The snowflakes falling gently down
And the holly on the tree

But which ever season that you call
Thy will it must be done
When my life on Earth is over
When you call, then I must come

E M Eden

AUTUMNAL MORNINGS

Dank, dark and misty mornings
    The grass all wet with dew
Hedges hung with ripened fruit
    Star spangled webs all new.

The lazy sun ascends the sky
    Casting a soft mellow glow
It warms the land and harvest field
    Where gentle breezes blow

Bright cold and frosty mornings
  The grass all crisp and white
The leaves all yellow red and gold
  Fall to form a carpet bright.

The land prepares for winter's rest
  After yielding forth its goods
But even now beneath the earth
  Are forming next year's buds.

Pat Vivian

THE HILL

Towering above like a giant praying,
This work of God before me laying,
Stretching out in front it seems forever,
To remind me how God can endeavour.

Grass as green as an Emerald sea,
Flowing in wind for all to see,
Garlands of primrose scattered round,
Bluebells abundant on the ground.

Trees like antlers grow on high,
They almost seem to touch the sky,
Their branches full of buds so green,
Standing so tall as if in a dream.

Clear water icy cold like glass,
Trickling over craggy rocks on way past,
Grass like a skirt right to the girth,
Hemmed by the water rims of a skirt.

Angela S Hitt

THE GLEN

Grasshoppers sizzle
Bright butterflies and bees
Court harebell and campion
And pockets of purple prepare
The hills of heather.

Lively streams flow secretly,
'neath network of warm grasses
And freshen arid places,
Continual in their constancy.

Animals both black and white,
Cow and sheep together meet,
Ruling over their domain,
Contented, fed on hill and plain.

The air pure, engulfing,
Precious and protected,
With sweet smell of nectar
Faintly rising.

How can we hold and keep this majesty?
Wanderers on the way,
Perhaps even thou doth bow
To thy Creator
With each passing day.

Carry Aubrey-Fletcher

SPRINGTIME

Sing a song of springtime,
      Birds upon the wing,
All the earth rejoices,
      In the call of spring.

There is no time like springtime,
      Take a walk in the garden and look,
You will find a little snowdrop
      Hidden in a shady nook.

This small and dainty blossom,
      As white as the driven snow,
Is the first of springtime flowers
      That in our gardens grow.

Soon we shall see the crocus
      In mauve or golden dress,
And if the sun is shining
      Open their petals to feel its caress.

The stately daffodil follows on,
      How beautiful they shine,
Like a trumpet, sounding to greet the spring,
      Giving glory to our God divine.

The trees in winter, stand stark and bare,
      Are suddenly covered in green.
What a joy to live in the country,
      And gaze on this beautiful scene.

The little birds are building their nests,
      Or feeding the baby ones,
We hear the bird song all day long,
      As the earth is filled with new birth.

Beautiful, beautiful springtime.

Dorothy Turner

SOUNDS OF BEAUTY IN NATURE

A baby's chuckle holds such joy,
Full of love with smiles so coy,
Singing waters in a rippling stream,
Inducing sleep with a peaceful dream.

Wind rustling o'er a field of corn
Like waves on the shore in early morn.
Winds gently blowing in the trees,
And gentle humming of the bees.

The patter of sweet summer rain,
Gently tapping on your window pane,
Or the sound of a tempest at night,
With thunder and lightning to show God's might.

Chestnuts cracking on a log wood fire,
Adds a taste to your hearts desire.
Mooing cows in meadows green,
Adds to the beauty of the scene.

There's thousands of sounds for us to share,
Look around, sound is everywhere.
I thank the Lord that I can hear,
His gift of Nature's sounds so dear.

Leonard Townsend

SEASONS

The sky is clearly blue in the springtime of our lives.
As children days are endless, hopes are high.
The need for us to know, to find out how and why,
As wondrously reflected in the eagerness of eye.

In summer we are rushing headlong on our way,
No time to sit and wonder as long as needs are fed,
We grasp at every straw as if it were our last,
No thought about the future for now the colour's red.

The colour's rich and deep in the autumn of our days,
Experience has taught humility,
We fear onset of winter, the river deep and wide,
Remember springtime's eager rushing tide.

And yet the tree in winter, devoid of all its leaves,
Stands in such stark beauty against a leaden sky,
Its purpose is fulfilled, it's born the fruits of life,
Its children look to springtime, with a yearning how and why.

Christine Lockton

LIVING WATERS

Is life like a tide,
Turning every day,
Bringing unforeseen currents,
Tossing stormy seas,
Or calm and mellow sunsets,
Changing to a soft contented breeze?
You see the pebbles on the shore,
Of different shape and form,
Some may be discoloured,
Some sparkling like new.
But God is part of them,
And sees them, just as he sees you.

So please don't be discouraged,
When things don't go your way,
For the cloud of rain will soon disperse,
The sea will rise again,
And you will, gently drifting,
Find your crystal bay.

J Beaumont

I LOVE RAINBOW BIRDS - (EUROPEAN BEE-EATERS)

A floating liquid call.
Early morning. Mallorca.
The Rainbow Birds fly south
singing their welcome songs,
          I wish you Rainbow music.

Their plumage sparkles
like a treasury of jewels:
topaz gleams to amber,
emerald sheens to sapphire,
          I wish you Rainbow colour.

Like guardian angels
full of grace, silhouettes
against the sky, they fly
to bring renewing joy.
          I wish you Rainbow grace.

Val Osmond

A PERFECT SETTING

It's calm here under the tree cover
As I waste this time the foliage discovered
The crows and rooks to name a few
Oh how I admire this wonderful view

The only thing evident to my surprise
A funeral mobile of peculiar size
The tree top commotion dawns another day
Just one of those things I had to say

Tantalising branches amazes curiosity
As I watch in awe it's not so costly
It's so beautiful just being here
No other feeling makes me secure

J P Sutton

LEAVES

Where does a leaf fall?
Is it carried by the wind
To lay on some field
To dry and crack?
Does anything ever bring it back?

Perhaps an unknown hand
Will gently reach to pick the leaf
And take it to the others
Do leaves have sisters, brothers?

Maybe the springtime burst of leaves
Each miracle upon the trees
Are re-incarnated in some way
To enjoy another day

Maureen Finch

WHO CAN DOUBT?

The wonder of a snowflake falling
The clear notes of a blackbird calling
To watch a sunset all enthralling
Who can doubt the love of God?

The flowers with petals softly curling
New leaves upon the trees unfurling
The waters in the rivers swirling
Who can doubt the love of God?

The scent of each fragrant flower
Each pleasant sunny summer's hour
All to the glory of His power
Who can doubt the love of God?

Molly Rodgers

THE HARVEST

Harvest Festival is here again
When we thank God for the grain
For all His mercy, love and care
He has shown to us with no mean share
We thank Him for our health and strength
For fruit that is harvested at length
For all good things we take for granted
Grown by Him but by us planted
Dear God, open up our eyes
That we may truly realise
The unseen gifts bestowed as well
More valuable than words can tell
Food for the soul as milk and honey
Far more valuable than money
Let us acknowledge and use them right
Bring them out into the light
Dear Lord, help our infirmity
That we may dwell with Thee in Eternity.

Evelyn A Evans

GOD MADE THIS WORLD FOR ALL

God made this world for all
For the flowers birds and bees
He gave us day, He gave us night
God made this world for our delight.

God made this world for all
For children big and small
God made this world for all to see
God made this world for you and me.

Lynda Bontoft

88

FROST

Nature's icy fingers
spiking grassy tips
Just for a while
all is white.

Triumphant sun -
glinting, searching, melting
Reaching down with golden fingers -
making all things green.

Elizabeth Borresen

THE SHAPE OF GOD'S NATURE

Look for pleasure in the lines of shape,
Look for beauty in the curves of nature.
In the cone of a limpet or a scallop's fan
The periwinkle spirals as only it can.
A rectangular razor, sharply honed,
Chameleon colours finely toned.
The dome of a jelly fish flaps about
Like a storm-shocked umbrella, inside out.
A starfish glides with pentagonal pace -
To oar obliquely in the off-shore race.

Sharp silhouettes in a storm-ridden sky,
The arc of a wing as sea-birds cry.
Black cormorants hunch on a rock to dry,
So waterlogged, they cannot fly -
Like a gossip of old men, passing by.
As question marks the swans' neck bend
Posing the riddle that has no end.
Look for pleasure in the lines of shape,
Look for beauty in the curves of nature.

Gilolden

WALKING WITH GOD

Our lives can never be the same
When we have walked with God.
When he has called us by our name
When he has taken all our shame
When he has said, for us He came
We choose to walk with God.

Sometimes we turn the other way
Where once we walked with God.
We do not talk to him each day,
We do not care, forget to pray,
We carry on in our own way,
Forget to walk with God.

But oh, his love is ever true
He says my child, I died for you
I've called you, saved you, you are mine,
and even when you're out of line
I'll gently lead you, guide your way
And very soon will come the day,
Again, you'll walk with God.

When my quiet voice you'll surely hear
You'll want to walk with God.
And when I tell you 'Never fear'
And when for you I dry each tear
You then will feel me very near
I've led you back to God.

Mary Jones

AT THE SOURCE

There's a story that is not often told
How a bird at the source of the stream
Warned that clear water flowing lower down
Was not all it was made out to seem

The picnic in the forest was great fun
For this family it was their first
They had taken a hamper with plenty of food
But they had not catered for thirst

The water in the stream was so clear
They were tempted to drink to their fill
But ere they could start they were stopped on the brink
By a bird with a call loud and shrill

It was a bird with a plumage so bright
And a call one could never ignore
It came in the midst interrupting the scene
This bird they had not seen before

Then quickly it flew up the stream
The family thought again of their thirst
But as soon as they attempted to drink once again
The call came just as at first

They followed the stream to its source
And saw poison had been found by the bird
They forsook the drink but heeded the call
Of the One who desired to be heard

The source of the poison is the devil
The source of the stream is God's word
The family are those made by the hands of our God
Who desires that His voice may be heard

John Remmington

MY GARDEN

My garden is full of wonderful things,
The little fountain that trickles all day.
The birds swoop down to quench their thirst,
They don't really have time to stay.

The roses with colours so bright and bold,
Will lift their face to the sun.
To dry the dew from the morning mist,
As the new and beautiful day has begun.

The rockery stands proud and strong,
In a little corner all on its own.
The plants are tall and firm at the top,
Some trailing gently over the stone.

In a shady corner out of the sun
Grow the beautiful soft swaying ferns.
So gentle and graceful they play in the breeze,
Like children dancing in turns.

The willow tree is tall yet weeps
As it gazes all around.
She seems to say 'I'm in charge around here'
While her fingers caress the ground.

Now the evergreen hedge stands in guard of the place,
His coat is always soft green.
The winds try to push through and break him
But not a gap as he stands can be seen.

So last thing at night when I close the gate
And rest a while on the old wooden seat
I look around at my beautiful garden,
For one day the creator I will meet.

Cassarnda Bailey

IN QUIETNESS AND CONFIDENCE . . .

The trees in dignified silence stood
Surrounding the fields so green
While the sky came down with a gentle touch
Could this be the artist's dream?

The tiny cottages standing by
Are there many folks living there?
Is their place of life much slower than ours
And have they less worry and care?

The narrow road slowly winding its way
And the birds singing softly - yet sweet.
While the village church in the distance there
Makes this country scene complete.

May I keep within me forever
This image of quiet and calm
And to my soul's agitation
May it come as a healing balm.

Jean Hudson

IN GOD'S GARDEN

In God's garden grows a flower
fairest white, with sweet perfume
'tis the lily God created for men's
souls to save and cure.

In God's garden grows a flower
in my heart the fairest bloom
I will tend it while I live
and heaven's reward will be my joy

Jennifer Crawley

REFLECTION

Rest for a while by a crystal-clear lake
Fringed by a graceful network of trees
Their green reflection mirrored in the water
Will give your mind comfort and ease.

Walk for a while in a shady woodland
With ferns and bracken beneath your feet
Gaze up with wonder at the mighty oaks
Whose branches form an arch as they meet.

Pause for a while in a sunlit meadow
To savour the fragrance of new-mown hay
Rise early to hear the sweet bird-song
From the hedgerows at the break of day.

Linger for a while on a grassy bank
Where a silver stream flows gently by
As the scent of wild flowers fills the air
Under a blue and cloudless sky.

Sense for a while the presence of God
In your heart and in your mind
For His hand has created the beauty
In the quiet places that you find.

Joyce Bushby

FRUITFUL TREES

Let us be like fruitful trees
Planted by your hand;
Rooted firmly in the truth,
Upright here to stand.

Arms upheld in worship
Receiving your love-light:
Sending prayers like green leaves
Which wave at Heaven's height.

In storms of tribulation
Never to be thrown;
Our roots going deep in Jesus
In whom we first were sown.

Bearing fruits of holiness,
That all may taste and know;
How good and holy is the Lord
Who caused these trees to grow.

J Pollock

THE CROSS WE BEAR

Many things we bear in life,
From the cradle to the grave,
Our individual experiences
In the life our Creator gave;

Some crosses they are heavy,
Some crosses they are light,
But the most important thing,
Is the strength of will to fight!

With muscle of endurance,
Strong bones of faith,
With cartilage of devotion,
And mentality of praise!

If not in early years,
The latter then will know,
For no-one can succeed in life,
Without trials here below

Take courage then to bear the cross,
Be it heavy, or be it light,
Then with great honour you will find,
Joy! With a victorious life!

Esther Armstrong

MY PRAYER

I have often looked unto the sky
With many a tear wet in my eye
Asking God to hear my prayer
I need you Lord, are you there?

The still small voice would answer me
Yes My child can't you see, I am waiting,
Waiting, silently, My arms are wide my
Refuge free, come My child try not to
Struggle, the grass is green there is no
Rubble, My garden only holds the best,
Those who love Me will be blessed, peace
And joy, abundant love is what I hold for
You above, while you live on earth let Me be
Your guide, and one day in heaven to be at My side,
There in My garden, beauty serene, flowers and trees
Are evergreen.

Ruth McIntyre

SUMMER STORM

A moment ago the sky was blue,
The apple trees still, where the sun shone through
The peaceful garden, gay with flowers,
Promised me many lazy hours.

The sky turned black, as clouds appeared,
The driving rain, the garden cleared.
A madcap wind blew fiercely round,
The apples crashed down upon the ground.

Then, suddenly, all was peace again!
The sun came out: the driving rain
Stopped lashing out at flowers and trees;
The wind changed to a gentle breeze!

Nora D Jones

SENSE OF WONDER

Can you hear
the angels whisper?
Can you feel it
in the air?
Can you feel
a sense of wonder?
Can you hear it
everywhere?

Can you feel
the demons' anguish?
Can you taste it
in the air?
Can you taste
the sweetest victory?
Can you feel it
everywhere?

Can you touch
the edge of heaven?
Can you feel it
everywhere?
Can you sense
Christ's awesome presence
as our voices
fill the air?

C Arthurs

TO CAROLINE (OUR SECOND GRANDAUGHTER)

All summer long
The days lay quiet and waiting
Subdued deep-muted
Yet soft aware
That through the throng
Of autumn's terminating
In wonder rooted
You would be there.

So now we watch
In these the gentle fledgling days
The quiet slow smile
The gestures made
And there is much
That may reflect your later ways.

Our shadowed world
Will need the gilding that you bring
And as years mature
Time well may seek
Your song far-hurled
To speak anew of peace and spring
When night's dark endures
Or days are bleak.

Then shall this small child's hand
Lead again to the promised land
And her small voice suffice
To find once more the long lost Christ.

Claude H Bigg

THE SHOOT

Death came to our wood today.
The dawn had glowed
with touch of gold.
Shafts of sunlight
glanced upon our plumage,
making us one with earth
bracken and fallen leaf,
in glory of winter colour.

Suddenly harsh voices
broke the stillness.
Dogs barked, shots cracked -
bodies fell to earth
with dull thud
and moments later
lay in sodden heaps.

Shall man forever mar
the beauty of creation?

Margaret E Williams

THE ANIMAL KINGDOM

It snowed on the route to Christendom,
the magi's channels blocked.
They had globed their way to arctic climes
for the destiny no-one clocked.
Polar bears, affectionate,
played in the icy floes.
And there Christ's love of animals still grows.

Paul Kearns

THE WORLD

I sit here and I'm wondering
About the world which we live in
Why is it here?
Who made it?
And why to humans was it given?
The grass is so green and plentiful,
The trees so tall and strong
The years man has lived on this earth
Have been so very long
The sun so bright and golden -
Without this we could not survive.
The water, crops and animals -
On which all humans thrive.
The hot, the cold and of course the wind -
Who created all these things?
Why have some animals got four feet-
And why have birds got wings?
Why are we born when we're young
But die when we grow old?
As we learn more about this earth -
No doubt the story will unfold.

Heather Johnston

AUTUMN

The warmth of autumn sunshine
The beauty of the trees
The colours in the hedgerows
The passing of the bees
The end of all the harvesting
The farmer now at ease
The joy awakened in my heart
At visions such as these

Alan Duggan

100

MAKING SENSE OF LIFE

Look up, look up and see the sky,
Blue with the radiance of heavenly light.
Life-giving, life-sustaining radiance,
A gift of love, the gift of sight.

Then listen hard and hear the birds,
With heavenly song uplifting, cheering,
Chattering, whistling, cawing, cooing,
A gift of love, the gift of hearing.

The sounds we make, the way we talk,
Communicate, care, console, and teach.
The words that can express thanks for
A gift of love, the gift of speech.

For all our senses which we take
So much for granted all our days
Let's stop and think and use them right
As instruments of thanks and praise.

That praise might reach beyond the sky
Where angels sit with radiant faces
Echoing; re-echoing joyous praise,
Resounding through the heavenly places.

May those deprived of senses, Lord,
Be compensated from above
By the greatest gift You can bestow,
A gift of love, the gift of love.

Help us to trust that love each day,
Acknowledging the sins of man;
But confident that faith can make
Our lives, corrected, fit His plan.

A Stewart

THE NATURAL WORLD

Out in the country all nature stirs,
The wind in the willows, the song of the birds;
Starlight recedes from a new morn begun
With the freshness of dew and the dawning sun.

Awake all you people! See the natural world,
The greatness of all our God has unfurled:
Green is the grass and buds on the trees,
And birds flying swiftly on the soft gentle breeze.

Look out of your window, look into the sky,
Watch the sun fading from clouds rolling by.
Who was it said: 'There is no God?'
Could humans create the skies and the sod?

The flowers in the fields, the wildlife so free,
The sheep with their lambs, the small busy bee;
Our God the Creator has not worked in vain,
As Christians praise Him with so much to gain.

He gives us the love we share with each other,
The beauty of nature for all to discover.
Following Christ means we understand
The mysteries created by God's mighty hand.

Eileen M Chamberlain

WALK THE BEACH

Walk the beach,
Feel the sun touch your face,
Stop and survey the horizon
See the beauty of God's creation.

Walk the beach,
On a quiet summer's day
And feel the worries of living
Just fade away.

Walk the beach
On a summer's day,
And get His help as you go forward,
In the worldly rat race.

Walk the beach,
Feel the freedom,
Feel the peace,
Thank God there is such a place.

William Baker

ENJOYING HIS PRESENCE

Coming down the hill together,
Step by step, like sheep.
Walking sideways, stumbling, sliding,
Stopping for a break.

Quietly now, no time for talking.
On again, in fits and starts,
Admiring views not seen before
In foreign parts.

Jumping, scrambling, walking,
Wading through the streams,
Ankle deep in bogs and marshes,
Endlessly it seems.

Golden bracken, purple heather.
Contrasting hues, yet blending.
To all of nature's landscape
Their beauty lending

Dodging boulders, going down
Deep in conversation.
Walking peacefully home together,
Content in our creation.

Catherine Falconer

SPRING FAITH

Spring brings out the beauty of God's wonderful world;
She heralds the coming of summer.
She shouts forth her praise of God's wonderful work,
Of His glory she tells in full colour.
She faithfully follows the long winter months
When our hearts, like the days, can grow drear.
God's faithfulness proved by that first snowdrop shoot
That His purpose will work through the year.

Margaret Chappell

SCOTLAND

I must confess how beautiful this land of Scotland is:
Woodland trees of evergreen cluster on the hills - valleys too;
Dales and glades are carpeted with emerald hue,
'Mid which a stream meanders here and there
Reflecting silver-blue.
Cattle graze on pasture, while flocks of sheep unattended
Dot the undulating earth like snowballs on a verdant sea of grass
So peaceful, unpretentious.

Homesteads grace the landscape, and from distant view
In miniature perspective, appear like dolls' castle houses -
Some elegant, and of poor structure quite a few.
Ruins of ancient monuments, turreted edifices, tell a history true
Of a race of Northerners -
Hardy, strong, courageous, humorous too,
Inhabiting this realm of highlands, lochs and glens,
Undaunted through and through!

Were I to go on holiday, 'tis Scotland I would choose.
Could eye perceive such vista of grandeur in tranquillity
Contrasting in an age of uncertain rest
Beauty, peace and splendour at its very best

Jeannie Hay

A SPECIAL GIFT

God picked a pretty flower
In his garden up above
And sent it to the earth below
A gift of joy and love
A perfect little rosebud
Petal smooth her skin
Hair as soft as thistledown
Brown as a sparrow's wing
Eyes as blue as summer skies
With tiny hands and feet
A tender plant for loving care
A baby girl - so sweet

Wendy Castling

NATURE'S WAY

New shoots arise out of winter.
New life comes out of the dead.
Nature reveals her own glory.
Gives us a pathway to tread.

There is a pattern to nature,
Which gives us a pattern for life.
To help us to live with our problems,
Reducing perpetual strife.

All things will come out in due season.
Things will work out, given time.
Patience is always rewarded.
And sense comes with reason and rhyme.

When we can work out the rhythm,
And follow it out in our lives.
Then we have discovered the secret
By which Mother Nature survives.

Jean B Scott

THE MEADOW

There is a tranquil meadow where peaceful waters flow,
Where all is still and quiet, as if blanketed in snow.
My spirit guides escort me, when of material woes I tire,
Then gently calm and soothe me and dampen down my fire.

Come with me to the meadow, you're welcome any day,
Come see the beauty, feel the peace and watch the children play.
Their innocence and laughter is most joyous for to see,
And the meadow is quite big enough for you, the world and me.

For all the world is spirit and The Great One is within.
His love is big enough for all and can't be touched by sin.
If we can strive for goodness and spread the love around,
Then man will live in harmony, with His protection he'll surround.

V Francis

MIST TO END

The morning mist
echoed from the hills,
down to the valleys,
way below,
and God in His silence,
And God in His wisdom,
and God in His knowledge,
let all people know,
that surely, entirely and to all
in His land,
His beauty He'd give them
till each met their end.

J Callinan

LOOK AROUND

When you're feeling really down
Take your time to look around
The colours of our land so green
There's so much beauty to be seen.
Above a sky of brilliant blue
Leaves that sparkle wet with dew.
A ray of gold shining bright
And silvery stars light up the night.
Birds that sing a merry tune,
Flowers fragrant with sweet perfume.
Rain God send to quench the earth
The miracle of each new birth
All this and more
Is given free
To us for all eternity.
So when you're feeling really down,
Just take your time
To look around.

Paula Cronick

MYSTERY OF A BUTTERFLY

How you flutter by, butterfly
It's a mystery how you fly.
With pretty decorated wings
And your silent wing-beat.
It makes me wonder
How you flutter by, butterfly.
Maybe some day I will find out.
Maybe you will tell me today
Or another day,
Butterfly that flutters by.

Naomi Hannah Cumberland

THE FLEDGLING

While out on a Sunday morning walk, I saw a fledgling
lying on the cold, unrepentant stone that had taken its
life away. Eyes that would never have a chance to
open; like a still-born child that would never see its
mother's face; gaping mouth waiting to receive. A
lamenting mother watching helplessly from an empty
nest. A season's work over. Her untiring efforts to
bring her offspring to fruition stop here. She feels
alone in her agony of grief. Then, from St Andrew's
Church nearby, the bells begin to ring, raining down
reverberating sound, penetrating her silent trauma,
falling on the blessed and bereft alike. They sang as
they had never sung before and, with ears once deafened
with sorrow, she listens and hears the preacher's voice
riding on the wind, saying 'Not one sparrow falls to
the ground without your Father knowing.' She looks to
Heaven and speaks 'Will you remember my little
sparrow, Lord ?' Then she flies away into the future,
and another season.

Joan L Hill

GOD'S WONDERFUL WORLD

I cannot see You Lord and live,
For the brightness shines too brightly,
Thoughts cannot be spoken nor touched.
For we do not know, but guess
What beauty is outside nature,
Ineffable, transluminous,
Beyond Alpha and Omega,
Absolute beyond Absolute.

Dorothy Ann McGregor

UNTITLED

Hedges of green,
Trees that are tall,
These wonderful gifts,
God gave to us all.
Carpets of bluebells,
And primroses yellow,
We find in the woods
Just over the meadow.
Don't pass them by,
As though they weren't there,
But linger a while,
To thank God in prayer.

L McCarthy

THE WIND

The wind today, a gentle breeze,
That softly whispers, through the trees,
And woos the flowers with sweet caress,
And stirs the grass with gentleness.
But yesterday - a savage roar,
That dashed the waves upon the shore,
As dangerously - the boats were tossed
And many with their crews, were lost.
On changing wind, capricious swain,
That courts the sunshine, and the rain,
Be kind today and bring to me -
My own beloved, home from sea.

Margaret Brassington Griffiths

WINTER LANDSCAPE

Thank You for colours, Lord! I saw today
The seagulls flash, like scimitars of white against the grey.
Then, sweeping down, they lighted on the land
Like snowy pearls across the earth's dark throat,
Strung there by Your dear hand.
Jackdaws hopped in the stark boughs, uttering harsh greeting,
Nudging each other, looking grave - like old men at a Board Meeting!

Thank You, Lord, because You never count the cost
Of making Your world beautiful: grass, stiff with frost -
A million blades to make one lawn
Outside our window - sparkling in the dawn
And lovely, to behold.
Later, the blue-green blades were tinged with gold
As the sun warmed them.
(Like Your smile so often melts my grief, Lord. I love you so!)

You are so open-handed, Father!
It would be greed to ask for more than simple things to meet my need.
Yet You pour into my lap so many joys.
Unsearchable riches in my dear Jesus!
Flowing,
    Welling up,
        A Niagara of love!

A cornucopia of all You are -
    My bright and morning star,
        My dawn,
            My sun,
                My quiet peace at dusk,
                    My guardian through the night,
                        My dear delight!

Pauline F Hillier

BURDENS LIFTED

We've no need to walk in darkness,
For Jesus is our light
If we just trust our way to Him,
Then He will make it bright.

Just give Him all your problems,
Your worries fears he shares,
And leave them in His mighty hands
He understands and cares.

For everyone is special
As Jesus loves us all,
And we will find Him waiting,
To answer when we call.

So don't keep on your worrying,
Which tears the soul apart,
Just leave it with our Father
And *trust* His loving heart.

J Tolhurst

GOD'S WONDERFUL WORLD

I woke this morning and what did I see
The most wonderful sight that beheld me
The blue of the sky the song of the bird
The most beautiful sound that I've ever heard
I looked to the ground and there I could see
God's beautiful flowers were smiling at me
The trees they swayed gently to the breeze
Bowing so serenely for everyone to see
I turned my head up towards the skies
And thanked the Lord for the sight before my eyes
For this is God's wonderful world made for you and me
So all of us can enjoy and all of us can see.

Elizabeth Leach

UNTITLED

Dear heaven rain down soft sounds
upon the earth.
Seeds lie broken-hearted there, unseen.
Quench rapacious cushioned green.
Wash them in a timely hour.
Embedded flower, and me.

Jarn Duncan

WONDERS OF THE WORLD

In my solitude, I sit and dream,
Of all the wonders I have seen.
The beauty of an early dawn
Where the golden sunrise greets the morn.
The chorus of the little birds, a joy to hear.
O thank you God for giving me ears.

I awake from my slumbers and look around.
At the beautiful flowers that carpet the ground.
The silence broken by a bee in flight
O thank you God for giving me sight

I arise and walk through the fields so green
So many wonders again to be seen
The sheep and cattle grazing quietly there
Enjoying themselves without a care
Bleating now and then as if to greet
O thank you God for giving me feet.

Thank you God for giving me birth,
And the many wonders of the earth
Without your aid there wouldn't be
These many wonderful things I see.

Eirwen A Jones

POIGNANT

Streaming came the teardrops
Falling like the summer rain
Each one a salty globule
Each one a cry of pain
Her fragrant hanky folds them in
To be treasured and put away
Each drop a poignant memory
Of the days that used to be
She remembers the days
When you romped with the dog
And caressed the garden flowers
Tempted the blue-tits
With pieces of cheese
Oh, happy, happy hours
Now no more the cuddles and kisses
No more the walks in the rain
Just the memories lingering on
Each one a cry of pain
Time will heal the loss she feels
But the pain she must now bear
She knows the tears will flow again
Like the rain that's always there
But in the good Lord's garden
Whose flowers for you now thrive
Those memories of her yesterdays
Will keep her love alive.

Charles Omer Desjarlais

RENEWAL

I see you in the clear,
running water;
I feel you in the grass,
wet and soft underfoot,
I sense you in the clear,
deep, blue sky;
I hear you in the song
of the bird, waking from
winter;
I see you in the soft
haze of the new sun;
I feel you in the crisp
new morning emerging
from the long winter grey;
I sense you in the pure
white of the young flower;
I hear you in the breeze
gently rocking the first
green leaves.

Kerry Webb

GOD'S WONDERFUL WORLD

When I wake up each morning to the singing of the birds,
I feel a marvellous pleasure; I'm glad to be of worth.
No matter if it's raining, or if the sun shines bright,
I thank God I am living in this wonderful place called earth.

As the hot afternoon sun beats down on me,
And the bees buzz and fly from flower to tree;
I gaze at the scene spread out before me,
And marvel at such wonderful beauty.

When the cool evening shadows fall,
And the lowering sun overshadows all;
There's still so much beauty all around,
Full of heavenly, wonderful sound.

At last, when darkness covers the land,
I pray that God will hold me in his hand,
So that I might, once more, greet the dawn,
And look forward, with hope, to a wonderful morn.

Ruth Lydia Daly

STAR GUIDE

Look up at the stars,
Shining with white brightness
In black skies.
Tiny, twinkling points
Of white light;
And one brighter
And whiter
Than all the rest.
The Polar star -
Star of the ships:
Guide of the navigators
Of seas and wide oceans.
Steady and bright,
It is always there,
Always . . .

And thus it is
In all nights,
And in all darknesses
There is always the one
Who will show the way.

Mary Fawbert Wilson

THE ORCHESTRAL AIR OF THE RIVERSIDE

The murky water, still when nothing stirs,
Laps the collapsing bank as river craft pass by:
The tell-tale ripples of surface activity;
While down below, where human sight cannot pierce,
Escaping air bubbles effervescently to the surface
And entertains thoughts of a busy grimy world.

The lush moss and grass of the bank
Give shelter to beetles, ants, and like creatures;
Though further along this stretch of water
Reeds and long grass become the hide-out of larger species.
The moor-hen nests here; where she feels safest;
But the water-vole chooses a hole in the bank.

The old deformed oak, leaning heavily upon the wind,
Arches its back to shadow the saplings
And the well-trod bridle path that meanders with the river
To its wide lowland outlet at the coast.
In contrast, the weeping willow trails its foliage in the water
Like a small child does its extremities over the side of a boat.
A picnicking family entering the picture - as yet incomplete -
Produces a discord, thus resultant disharmony.

Tobias Gregg

TO EVERYTHING THERE IS A SEASON

Sitting in a garden on a summer afternoon
Enjoy each lovely moment, for winter comes so soon.
Close your eyes and drift away on the warm sweet scented air.
And listen to the sounds of summer round you, everywhere.

The birds are lazy in the trees, nest building frenzy over
Bees buzz in the flower beds and sip from purple clover.
Far off, in the distance, someone mows the grass,
Close your eyes and drift away, for summer soon will pass.

Children's voices echo as they chatter at their play,
Happy in the freedom of their summer holiday.
That brown, bare-legged freedom remembered from the past.
Oh savour every moment children, summer days don't last.

Too soon the autumn leaves will fall and winter nips the toes,
The flowers die till all that's left is summer's faded rose.
But, we all can have that moment on a summer afternoon,
Be still, enjoy it while you may for winter comes too soon.

Valerie Burge

SUMMER

As I look around me,
On this summer's day,
I think of all the riches,
Before my eyes displayed.

The riches in the garden,
The grass, the plants, the trees,
The flowers nod, the grasses weave,
In gardens and in leas.

With all this blessed splendour,
Our heart with joy should ring,
And sing the praise of Him who died,
Our gracious saving King.

How often do we praise Him,
For such great gifts as these,
How often do we realise,
That we are rich indeed.

So I'll praise Thee ever Saviour,
For the gifts Thou has bestowed,
But chiefly for Thy saving presence,
In this sinful soul's abode.

B L Johnston

NATURE'S MUSIC

I sat and watched the ballet of the flowers
dancing to the music of a summer breeze,
Aided by orchestrations of the birds and bees
filling the air with perfume, song of showers.
In tune with the sigh of leaves in the trees
nature's music soothes the soul in troubled hours,
These are the moments of the day to pass
listening to the rustling rhythm of the grass,
Butterflies float on air in time to waving bloom
the honey bee enters the stage wings beating to the tune,
Webs of floating lace hang as if from the loom
a petal falls and drifts over garden like a balloon,
This overture to life a tribute to earth's powers,
what wonder to the eyes is the ballet of the flowers.

J Clarke

WHEN I SIT AND PONDER

When I sit and ponder,
On the beauty all around.
My heart is filled with love for Thee,
For all that You have given me.

The velvet petals on the flowers,
The blossom on the trees.
Birds hovering in the sky above,
Singing of Your precious love.

The sunshine and the falling rain,
The miracle of birth.
Earth and sky and rolling seas,
Thank you Lord for all of these.

J Hawkins

TREES

Where I can think - and
drip from leaves with rain - to the
ground's soul - peace at last.

Rhiannon

BEES

The buds on the flowers
     have opened wide
With plenty of room
     to get inside
Those beautiful blooms
     so full of nectar
A gourmet's feast
     for the flying sector
Of course I mean
     the wasps and bees
Which often have their nests
     high up in the trees.
It's fascinating to watch them
     toiling away so busily
And we know from experience
     nothing is as busy as a bee
They leave their nests
     in search of new ground
And when they find it
     they tell everyone around
By leaving a trail
     for others to follow
Then when the food supply is exhausted
     they start afresh on the morrow

Tom Sullivan

HEAVENLY SEASONS

Thank You Lord that I can see
The wonderful things that are around me
The daffodil with its bright yellow hue
Sunset at night, early morning dew

The spring shoots showing through so green
All around the flower buds can be seen
Everything so fresh and bright
Thank You God, it's such a delight

The blue sky and the summer sun
The shouts of children having fun
All of these things have been given by You
And I praise and thank You, I really do

In autumn the corn turns to a rich golden brown
The leaves from the trees come tumbling down
O Lord, there is so much that You have given
I am glad that You are up there in heaven

Ann Lyne

GOD'S MORN

Soft mist through trees
Bereft of leaves
Upon a winter's morn.
Sunshine so bright
Gets rid of night
Another day is born.
Frost quickly melts
And leaves droplets
That like jewels do adorn.
God's brand new day
Is on its way
Oh Blessed Creator's morn.

Maureen Mernock

CAPTURED BY MY CREATOR

When I have stood in a warm tropical rain,
that washed all coldness and doubt away;
when I have taken wings into Guatemalan hills,
that rose above the clouds in awesome beauty;
when I have watched the Niagara River,
fall off the edge of the world in grace and power;
when I have sailed mid-Atlantic skies,
that were the laser-lightening white of pure holiness;
when I have walked the knife edge of Cornish cliffs,
that cut into the sea with truth and sovereignty;
when I have sun-bathed in the back garden,
and awoken to see the complex simplicity of a daisy;
my soul has been captured,
enraptured by my Creator God.

Mark Roper

TREES

Depths of Beauty breathe
living prayers. Was there ever
such a time? Backdrops
to Humanity yield and sustain,
protect us unprotected. Living
Mysteries of cataclysmic hold.

Golden glow of withered expectation
leaves acknowledge our existence. Existential sometimes,
now perennial, in suffering yet are they
exultant, boundless,
graceful entities of power.
Life-giving forces
misunderstood. Agents
of Heaven. Our guardians.
Boundless. Bound. Yet Free.

Elizabeth Kerl

REVELATION

When I see a rainbow, crimson sunset, bright sunrise,
A starlit night, white fleecy clouds high in the Summer skies,
Hills and forests, mountains, green valleys spread below,
Lakes and streams and rivers, the ocean's ebb and flow,
I see in the Creator artist's eye, and sculptor's hand,
Such beauty could not happen, it was wonderfully planned.

Each time I hear a blackbird, a thrush or robin wing,
Or hear the pure ecstatic notes of skylark on the wing,
Or catch the sound of happy children laughing at their play,
Murmuring streams, whispering grass as breezes pass that way,
When words or music touch the soul and the heart is stirred,
In these and countless other gifts the Creator's voice is heard.

When I feel the freshness of a lovely day in Spring,
And feel the new re-surging life reviving everything,
And sense the resurrection taking place within the earth,
Nature responding at God's touch to its new rebirth,
Then I feel within my heart something of His power,
Some re-awakening of the soul in its resurrection hour.

Each time I touch the petal softness of a baby's skin,
Or pluck a fragile blossom, pink, rose, or frail jasmine,
Caress a baby's cheek or touch a loved one's hand,
Perhaps I am a little better able to understand
Just something of God's majesty, love and power and grace,
Revealed to us in human love, earth and sky and space.

When I see perfection in the beauty of a rose,
Something of its fragrance through my being flows,
Each time I see sweet innocence in a child's clear eyes
Shining with joy or wonderment, incredulous surprise,
Or feel the small hands of a child placed trustingly in mine,
I am drawn a little closer to the heart of the Divine.

Edith Stell

AUTUMN
(Dedicated to Sylvia my wife)

As autumn comes and colours change
It brings such difference in its range
Leaves falling trees looking bare
I can only stand and stare

Another miracle of nature upon this earth
But of seasons there is no dearth
Colours turn from green to brown
As the leaves come tumbling down

And as they fall with a hush
Everything goes that was so lush
But in due time it will come again
With spring and gentle rain

Let's not be sorry when it passes
For in spring comes new grasses
Buds will form and life will grow
Greenness will return to this world we know

So let's not mourn the falling leaf
Let not your heart fill with grief
Another season goes by
Soon to return with clear blue sky

Admire the colours as they change
It's just another different stage
A miracle in this marvellous land
So beautiful, so grand

Nature in its glory changes
Everything down through the ages
From green to brown and even red
Back to green for after all life goes ahead

Prince Rhan

THE BROWN WREN

The earth lies frozen and still, under
a blanket of crisp white snow
The flowers and shrubs lie asleep
in the winter gloom.
And yet life is alive in this garden of mine,
Today I was visited by a little brown wren,
Her visit brought a blessing to my heart,
She was a delight to my eyes,
As she hopped and skipped around,
with a nod of her little head.
First to the right, then to the left,
as she looked for her daily bread.
Soon she will take leave of me and my garden
My hope is that she will return again,
and maybe bring a little friend
And once more on a winter's day I
will rejoice, as I await the spring
and a new dawn.

M H Liddle

PEACE OF MIND

I know a cornfield where in summer
bright red poppies grow.
There the sun with dying splendour
sets the world aglow.

I know a thrush whose liquid music
echoes through the dell,
rising falling ever calling
in cascading swell.

I know a sea where waves are furling
white as the driven snow
gently rocking interlocking
in an endless flow.

I know a copse where I may wander
and a primrose find.
So with all these blessings
I can know true peace of mind.

Joan Breton

HIGH FLIGHT

I have slipped the surly bonds of earth
And danced the skies on laughter's silvered wings,
Sunward I've climbed and joined the
Tumbling mirth - of sun split clouds,
And have done a hundred things
You have not dreamed of,
Wheeled and soared and swung,
High in the sunlight lit silence
Hovering there,
I've chased the shouting wind along,
And flung my eager craft through floodless
Halls of air,
Up, up along the long delirious burning blue,
I've topped the windswept heights with easy grace,
Where never lark or even eagle flew,
And while with silent lifting mind I've trod,
The highest untrespassed sanctity of space,
Put out my hand and touched
The face of God.

Joan Smith

BEYOND REASON

The loom of wonder idle lies
No longer are the threads of mystery
                              and awe
which weave the rainbow, seen
For in the tapestry of life today -
                    the age of space,
the strands of marvel and surprise
                         are there no more.

For man has reached the moon
                    and his research
has shattered fantasies with facts -
                         or so it seems.
Yet there remain the poet, mystic
                    and the child
whose inner eye can still discover
                         miracles on earth
as fragile as the gossamer of dreams.

The glistening silver of the spider's web
The blue-green shimmer of the peacock's fan
The candled chestnut, and the pear-tree,
                    ermine-clad in May
are proofs of God's creative power,
                    which even man
with all His reasoning and His skill
                    cannot explain away.

Margaret Holmes

GOD'S WONDERFUL WORLD

Have you ever seen the wonder of God's world
Have you felt an exaltation when rising from
                                        your bed
When you greet the early morning to the chorus of the
                                        birds
And the hustle and bustle of life starts
Does the beauty go unnoticed as you hurry on your way

Or do you take the time to thank God and to pray

Have you gazed upon the sunset in the sky
At the close of day when all is very still
Has the wonder caught your breath and
have you ever wondered why
More people do not see the wonder of
God's world
In the winter there is beauty all around
For the icicles form patterns in the trees
But we hurry on to get out of the cold
So we miss the works of art that are made with nature's
                                        brush
Another way of showing God's beauty in the world.

I ask you friend be still awhile and pray, and you life will
be enriched beyond compare

Not with fast cars jewellery and fame
But with a peace and tranquillity that only
He can give and your eyes will be opened
To the wonder of God's world.

Joan Reeves

LOOK AND SEE

Have you ever really looked at trees,
Or studied clouds above,
Or gazed upon a little child,
Whose eyes are full of love?
Have you watched a little bird, as it flies, through the air
Or gazed upon a butterfly, as it rests without a care,
Have you seen all nature's colours,
As they change from day to day?
Seen the quickness of a tiny mouse
As it scurries on its way,
The tiny ant so busy, with his daily toil,
So many little creatures, that live in God's good soil

So many lovely things to see.
If you can just make time,
To stop, and look, and listen,
Just for a little while,
Have you seen a golden sunset,
As it slowly goes to rest
And watched the moon appear,
With stars, twinkling, at their best,

Have you thought how wonderful these gifts
                    Of the land, and sky, and sea?
Given with love, from *God* above,
                    For all eternity.

Jacqueline Claire Davies

GUARDIAN ANGEL

Contact,
Hold on tight for this flight.
We leave the air strip of green with soaring hearts.
An upward lift, skyward bound, far from the ground.
The wooden propeller speeding, round.

Skyride mist, the elixir of life, cutting through the frosty ice,
Passing the speeding aeronautics of torn billowing clouds.
Lunging into the vigorous nothingness abyss.
A wing and a prayer for those who dare.
'I will never leave thee, nor forsake thee.' Hebrews. ch.13.5.

The wonderful world of the elevated aviator.
Whisking whirlwind skyholes with double barrel heart rolls.
Swooping to looping loops.
Secured by a shadow and a strong seat belt.
No cockpit canopy for me, no parachute, what a hoot.

Thrown back into the seat by the shout of the wind.
Cold savage skies, wide opening eyes,
Enhancing and magnifying, all around vision.
With twin circle goggles the mind begins to boggle.
Solid and unyielding, the heavy flying jacket.

Shattering the silence, an airspace crescendo
Oscillating the vertical speed indicator.
Pulsing throttle roars of the screaming engine
Muffled by the soft leather flying helmet,
Flowing is the silken white trailing scarf.

Life is full of leaps and bounds
Ups and downs, spin rolls and side slip dips.
When you land upon the ground,
Even if you tumble and fall,
The Lord will be with you through it all.

Anthony Keyes

MY HEAVENLY GARDEN

Washing dancing happily in the breeze
Branches swaying, waving gaily in the trees
Roses nodding, with a gentle graceful ease,
The frolicking breeze playfully comes to tease,
Nature brings excitement with a joyous breeze.

Fluffy white clouds calmly float lazily through
The British sunny summer sky of azure blue,
The smooth green grass, smells fresh and new,
The freshly cut lawn spreads a peaceful hue
And a beautiful aroma wafts from red roses too.

Precious moments relaxing, in my garden 'neath the sun,
Pigeons cooing, birds tweeting, singing sweetly everyone.
My three tabby cats sleepily into the shade have gone,
For a siesta 'neath the bushes, curled up each one,
Inner peace and contentment had descended with the sun.

Linking with nature's beauty, I felt upliftment there,
With its movement, colour, perfume, and warmth so rare,
In my Heavenly garden I was privileged to share,
Where time seemed to stand still, and I had not a care,
Receiving healing, happiness, God's love was everywhere.

God's wonderful world in my garden I had found,
In the stillness of a summer day I sat and looked around,
Escaping TV's bad news with its monotonous sound,
Government leaders talk a lot, want power and the pound,
God's wonderful world will forever remain profound!

Stella Bush-Payne

MAN IN GOD'S WORLD

Wherever the eye seeks,
Mountain, towering peaks;
Glaciers and fjords;
A wondrous scene affords.
Man, on holiday, passes quickly by;
By coach or by boat - he even may fly.
Schedule to be kept - no time to wander;
Natural wonders, no time to ponder.
Take time to understand
These great wonders - and
As you thrill at the sight,
Marvel at nature's might.
For the awful power of creation
Should fill each man's heart with admiration.
The fleeting power of man pales beside
The lasting might of nature, beautified.
Stalactites, stalagmites;
Even more startling sights.
How long they take to form
Hidden from man-made storm.
To obtain fulfilment, no headlong rush,
Away from man's shrill noise, a quiet hush.
No hankering over fame or glory,
Content to let God write the true story.
The creatures that abound
In the sea or on ground,
And the birds in the sky
Capture the tourist's eye;
Can man find time to halt and realise
How humans appear in these creatures' eyes!

Roy Hammond

MEDITATION

One day I looked and perceived mountains tall.
Majestic and beautiful dressed in purple and green.
And I thought to myself where do I fit in?
Is there a place for me a human?

Then my eyes beheld a magnificent scene.
A powerful waterfall crashing into a stream.
And I thought to myself where do I fit in?
Is there a place for me a human?

Next I saw a seed coming to life.
To bring forth lovely flowers
No trouble or strife.
And I thought to myself. Where do I fit in?
Is there a place for me a human?

As I pondered I thought of the one who created it all
Including me.
Suddenly I knew beyond doubt, there is a place for me
For God in His infinite love.
Sent His Son Jesus from Heaven above.
To take all my sin at Calvary.
So that I could have a new life and be set free.
When the Lord calls me and my time on earth is o'er
Joyfully to Heaven my spirit will soar.

Isobel McDonald

GOD'S WONDERFUL WORLD

You created this wonderful world we live in
All those wonderful things that you created
To name just a few the flowers, trees, and the air we breathe
All the things that grow in the earth and live on the earth
When I see those birds in flight I say to myself how great it must feel to look
down upon this earth
The freedom they feel as they fly from the earth to the sky
For this inspires me to think of my Lord who created it all
for this is *God's* wonderful world

Those waterfalls that you created makes it all worth while
As we see what beauty the water falls in such a way
I stop and think there is no-one else who created such beauty
The trees as they wave about in the breeze with such great ease
Those fish and those creatures that swim around in your seas
This is His creation in *God's* wonderful world

Geraldine Perkins

THE BEAUTY OF CREATION

Thanking the Lord for all wonderful things,
God made all this earth and for this each bird sings.
Each flower bows down to the Creator above,
So peaceful is nature, like a single white dove.
The grass is so green and the sky yet so blue,
Thank goodness we know who to give all the glory to.
God reached down his hand and made all of the earth,
In just seven days, yet look at its worth.
Thanking the Lord for each life that he made,
He had each detail planned, so don't be afraid.
For each life that is lost, a new birth is found.
God continues to love us and the earth still goes round.
Instead of being sad, we must be thankful for this,
That the pleasure was ours, whilst on earth beauty lived.

Karen Mitchell

WE SIMPLY CAN'T COMPETE

The heavens they are a
      wondrous sight
A marvellous display
Of a brilliant designer's
      craftsmanship
On view night and day

Without a sound
Without a word
Silent in the sky
The sun moves out across
      The heavens
Giving life or all would die

It crosses the heavens
From end to end
And nothing can hide from
      its heat
However brilliant us humans are
We simply can't compete

The moon is there to mark
      the months
The sun to mark the days
He sends the light and darkness too
What a variety He has made

Christine Williams

JESUS IN NATURE

Come read of these words and you will surely see,
Things in creation God has for you and for me.
See even in nature He has placed His might,
Here are some examples written within your sight.

Like next to the nettle there is a dock leaf,
If you get stung then the dock will bring you relief.
When Satan attacks you causing you to sin,
Call on Jesus He will then cleanse you from within.

The plant life in blossom, yes it is unique,
To go and find it you will not have far to seek.
You can be grafted into 'The Tree of Life',
If you seek Jesus, He will take away all strife.

Look at the birds singing in the trees above,
Yes each one is chirping a melody of love.
The song they do sing is beautiful indeed,
They are praising the Lord for providing their need.

There's a fish that has a battle in its day,
It jumps over anything that gets in its way.
It jumps up waterfalls whether large or small,
Our God made the salmon an example to all.

When you're out walking this is what you can do,
Look at nature and see what God is teaching you.
Then pick up your Bible and read the Lord's Word,
You also can be lifted up, just like a bird.

Yes God's creation it's wonderful to see,
There are lessons to be learnt, yes lessons for thee.
When you come to the Lord and unto Him pray,
Just ask Him to teach you something on each new day.

Bill Going

MY GREATEST GIFT

I've walked along sun-kissed sandy beaches
Over tree-clad mountains reaching up so tall
Through lush green valleys with rivers gently flowing
These scenes of beauty I sit and now recall.

Down clay bank roads that had no visual ending
Tall grass blowing in the gentle breeze
To see the clear sky meet the blue-capped mountain
Hear the soft wind's pleasant sighing through the trees.

Endless gifts of beauty for men to cherish
Created with love and care for all to see,
No mortal hand could equal such creation
Such wondrous things bestowed to you and me.

As I recall the many joys created for us
Such wonders to be shared by one and all
I then recall the day I met my precious Saviour
Which for me 'twas the greatest gift of all.

Into my life He came with little warning
Oh! The joy that filled my heart and cleansed my soul
His presence and His love with me forever
Thank you! Jesus, for the day you made me whole.

Isaac Smith

ODE TO THE OAK

Giants of time unremembered
inspiring hope to preserve what we see,
in solid state your beauty lies
magnificent in nature's own glory.

Noble grandfather strong and proud,
in shades of earth your sturdy form
stands firm unmoved by elemental struggle
watching, reflecting through time.

Titan limbs of height and depths
grasp invisible threads of being,
crowned with emerald glory
your ancient vigil speaks true.

What fragments of lives do you see
in your ponderous study of life?
What flits before your sombre stare
belittled before your ancient grandeur?

Helen Saunders

PERCEPTION

Have you ever considered the spectrum,
The pleasure that colour can bring?
The power of perception is a truly remarkable thing.

Have you ever looked close at a flower,
Seen a rose through a drop of dew?
Have you ever crept up on a butterfly,
And pondered the symmetry of hue?

Take time to enjoy every colour
Beauty glows there in them all
From the fresh sparkling green of the springtime
To the deep mature shades of the fall.

If you add all the colours together
You will always end up with white,
And remember if you didn't have colour
You would be in perpetual night.

Colours relax, console and bring calm,
Utilize all the pleasures they bring,
The power of perception is a truly remarkable thing.

Gerald Finlay

A BREATH OF SPRING

Snowdrops peeping out of the ground
Daffodils dancing all around
Morning frost changes to morning dew
Signs of springtime to mention a few
The world suddenly seems a happier place
Birds singing, children playing smiles on each face
Spirits uplifted, life now has a reason
Springtime is such a beautiful season.

Betty Crawford

TRANQUILLITY

Sitting in the garden
on a warm summer's day,
so peaceful is this setting
let all worries fly away.

Both flora and fauna
are everywhere you see -
the beauty all around you
shines so wonderful and free.

Smiling faces flourish
in borders all around,
flowering so profusely
and in glory they are crowned.

Eyes are ever watchful
though rarely they are seen,
thriving in this paradise
camouflaged behind a screen.

Margaret Jackson

TAKE ME FURTHER . . .

Take me further to where the orchids grow free
And wild and sweet and perfectly pure
Where laughter shakes incense that wafts on the air
And dew on a petal is nectar to me.
Take me higher to where no other is found
But only your touch on a whispering wind
Where your loving is lifted from light on the leaves
Of trees that are dancing to each satin sound.
Then bathe me in waters of silvery streams
Caress me in rhythms thrilling and true
And cascading crystals will sprinkle the earth
In telling the beauty and oneness of you.

Virginia

PEACE

An ocean as it swallows setting sun
Beneath a fiery sky with gold-tinged cloud,
The pious innocence of praying nun
In humble purity, as she has vowed,
A mountain mirrored in a tranquil tarn,
The softness in the pink of Alpine glow,
The deftly moving finger working yarn,
Descent of waterfall in spate's full flow,
Siesta shade of summer leafy glade,
Two hearts which beat in harmony and love,
Sweet scent of hay that's fallen to the blade,
On frosty night the moon and stars above,
The gold and red of leaves before they fall,
Induce a sense of peace we comprehend;
But I believe one thing surpasses all -
The magic sound of voices as they blend.

Charles Povey

IMPRESSIVE WONDERS

I like to see a waterfall cascading from on high.
It's a magnificent sight to see
As it flows to the stream below.
Its regular, general motion
Adds more splendour to the rural scene.
Surely one of God's wonders
And a pleasure, you'll agree.

I like the great white horses
When a tide is at its height,
Bounding up towards the shore
And splashing against the rocks.
Another impressive sight to behold;
One more wonder of His might!

Another fascination for me
Are the clouds gliding by in the sky;
So delicate in formation,
Unique in every way;
Another instance of God's almighty hand
As they drift along on high!

Marjorie Cowan

TARN HOWS IN SUNLIGHT

Lost in a wonderland of woods, lake and hills,
Watching the ripples on the reed edged lake,
With majestic, brooding Conniston 'Old Man'
Smiling benignly on the sun-soaked trees.

This Lakeland gem was designed by Nature
But helped by man. The Divine result
Has revealed what our God with man can do,
That to the world God's love may show through.

See the tall pines whose sharp black shadows
Are climbing rocky, grassy hills;
See a lonely bird who sits so still,
Gliding the Tarn only for food.

I can only stand with in-drawn breath
When I'm looking down on such a view.
Words cannot tell of my inner glow,
In the sun, on Tarn Hows' pinewood slopes.

Sheila E Harvey

THE GROWINGNESS OF THINGS

The growingness of things
gives variability and change,
while at the same time, it is -
simple being.
Upwardness clambers for truth
below in dark and hidden silence.
Branches spread out meaning
and shelter for weak
forest animals. Mother
pours protection by green
pine needles.
Squirrels brood, rats
squirm, and dank
worm, voles and gannets
feed on each other.

All the time,
sunshine calls
the deep down growingness
of things.

L Ferguson

MY HOME - THE EARTH

His invisible qualities are clearly seen
by the wonderful creation all around - the
sky - sea - and land all made by a Master
enjoying his work - what joy he must have
had making a tree to stand the winds and rains -
the beautiful flowers that stand as a contrast
to the carpets of grass - winter - spring - summer
and the fall - all part of the Maker's Plan - yes your
works of wonder are clearly seen from the world's
creation onward.

R P Scannell

SEAGULL

Free as the wind
He was sailing the skies
Making me laugh
Then making me cry
Protecting or warning?
What then was his aim?
For, he did honour this mortal
Whose life, he had changed.
Filled with delight
Flames of fire, filled my eyes
As I begged him to rest
From his dance, through Paradise
Then following with pride
To the Heavens he soared
Free as the wind
To Eternity's door.

Irene Gunnion

A TIME TO TREASURE

Gazing idly from my door
I viewed the humpbacked bales of straw,
The hedgerows neat with berries flecked
Their rooted feet in flowers bedecked.

Waves of ivy tumbled over
Rusted plough knee-deep in clover,
Rooks and crows flew down to share
An old brick wall in need of care.

Small distant trees
Stretched on their toes
To reach the passing breeze that blows
Across the fields of long green grasses
Making ripples as it passes.

I spied a kestrel 'frozen high'
Begin to plummet from the sky,
Two long-eared rabbits, right on cue,
Trampolined themselves from view.

As if to make the scene complete
A passing lizard brushed my feet,
I turned,
The flowers' goodbye nod
Confirmed my faith,
There is a God.

G Price

SOUNDS COUNTRY

I wake each morning to country sounds,
The hooting owl, the baying hound,
A cockerel crowing, the church bell sounds,
Making me glad to be around.

This morning when at six I woke,
To animal sounds, not to folk,
The sparrows chirping, a donkey braying,
Hello, good morning, they were saying.

Tomorrow when at six I rise
What sounds will my ears surprise,
The pigeons cooing and foxes barking,
Telling me the day is starting.

N Griffiths

SWAN SONG

Life on the river
      Was gentle and serene
The young male swan came gliding
      Silent as a dream
'I won't turn back, I'll carry on'
      He made a firm decision
When just around the bed
      He was greeted with a vision
She looked so young and lovely
      Like a Swan Princess
He circled round and bowed his head
      Her wing tip to caress
Their courtship will last all their lives
      Their love will last forever
When two swans make a pledge of love
      Then only death can sever

Ysabel

NATURE'S WONDERLAND

From majesty of the mountain tops
We look and see the variety of crops
Shimmering below, Oh look! The lake.
In the valley I spot a lively corn crake.

Then a black cloud gathers overhead
The shower which threatened, its raindrops shed
With rain-hoods and macs we are prepared
We descend, discuss the beauty we shared.

Then look! In the distance what do we see?
A glorious rainbow o'er a distant tree,
Poppies red in a fields of corn
We soon forget the recent storm.

The waves splash steadily on the shore
On the sand, the litter left we deplore
Why do folk both young and old
Drop their rubbish all sorts untold?

Since we were young, folk untidy have grown
In their children's habits, the seed is sown
We forget all this, as we board a bus
To see woods, trees and the landscape so lush.

The countryside in word or story
We cannot describe its real true glory
The ferns, foxgloves, squirrels in tree
Things half the people never see.

They are always in too much of a hurry
Rushing here to there in such a flurry
If they would pause and look around
They would see and hear many pleasant a sound
So let us stop and take in the view
The wonders of nature they are ever new.

L E Blake

MY GRANDSON'S RAINBOW

We chanced upon a rainbow as we walked out of the wood
'Oh look Grandad' said my small grandson 'where is the pot of gold?'
I laughed as I swept him up in my arms to get a better view
'Well it's all around ' I answered and he really believed I knew
'Where is it then?' he asked me 'I can't see any treasure or gold.'
'Look around' I said 'at the precious things' and then this story I told:
God made the world so big and round with *blue* skies above and below
With rich brown earth and dark *green* trees and seas that ebb and flow
Violet mornings turn into *yellow* sunshine and fade into *red* and *orange*
                                                                    sunset
Followed by nights of deep *indigo* and the moon and stars are then lit
'Where did it go to?' my grandson now asked as the rainbow faded away
'I can't see it now are you sure it's still here?' he looked around in dismay
'Well sweetheart' I told him 'the rainbow's still there but the colours
                                                    now shine as one light
When they are all working together they shine better and even more bright'
He ran up the path shouting 'Rainbow I'm still looking for you'
I hope as he grows he'll remember our walks in the woods as I do
Maybe he'll know the secret of life and living in God's Wonderful World
And see each of the colours as people each a beautiful thing to behold
We all make up the rainbow and though we all have our own special light
When together we shine with a brilliance then living can be a delight
It takes many things to make the world complete and we must never forget
It's only by working together we can nurture it and protect.

Milly Holme

GOD'S GIFTS

How lovely to look at a garden with its blossoms fair
and bright.
To listen to birds in the tree-tops, so often hidden
from sight.
The sun shines warmly on faces, while the breeze it
softly stirs,
The bushes and trees round about us, and the tops of
the lofty firs.
God has given us so much beauty, and His love He
freely bestows.
So let us give thanks and acknowledge, from Him
all our blessing flows.

F L Brain

WELSH THEATRE

Drawn curtains divided
So our window unites
Nature's contribution
Of morning delights.

Numerous lambs dance free
But shadow mother sheep
Waking hours are busy
No time's lost to sleep.

Rich pastures, luscious green
An early bathing dew
Refreshment is offered
Our woolly crew.

Mouth-watering falls splash
Their thirst-quenching ballet
A taste of Swiss theatre
From our Welsh chalet.

Graham Barger

EACH DAY IS DIFFERENT

The sun goes down
The moon, stars, night gives way
To quiet night restful sleep
To renew again another day
Each day is different God did say
In the sunshine you must have grey
With the clouds there is a rainbow
All the colours nice and bright
In all these there is God's sight.

Elizabeth Docherty

HOW BEAUTIFUL OUR WORLD

Sunset over sea, my heart stands still!
The wind rustling leaves gives me a thrill.
Beauty of the rainbow arching the sky,
Song of the lark as it flies up high.

Stream running clear as it glides along;
The spread of oak trees large and strong.
And smell of rain falling on grass,
All these I love as on I pass.

God's wonderful world, given to all,
Small violets hidden near a wall.
White fluffy clouds in sky of blue,
For these we thank You to name but a few.

All men and women of every race
Should try to make this a perfect place;
Where beauty and love go hand in hand
For a peaceful world as sea laps land.

Doris Mitchell

APPRECIATION

Today I said a simple prayer for all wonders of this world that are great.
Thanked the Lord, everything he did create.
Sun moon stars sorrow laughter, pain.
Clouds thunder lightning, rain.
Beautiful daffodils, tulips, buds still to open.
Privileged live on this earth at this Sacred Easter
celebration.

Green fields, trees newly-planted some old proudly standing
tall.
Chickens hatching, animals, pets loyal, true.
Appreciate joy they bring. Oh! Lord Bless You.
Strength to parents, grandparents who work very hard,
family friends loving supportive good times, bad.
New bright beginning as we plan ahead.
Good health or the sick, presence always there,
Departed loved ones who climbed up, 'Golden Stair'.
Outstretched arms you really do care.

Young children parading. 'Easter bonnets'. Rolling eggs down
hills.
Gracious Lord I kneel, 'Forget you?' I never will.
Skills talents in each of us you sowed the seed,
repaying every day, 'daily deeds', on path you lead.
Jesus I salute you, love fills my heart.
When I think of all pleasures.
'Chosen for us all to take part.'

Dawn Constable

ASPIRATIONS

If daily life be like a poem
What tune doth it set?
People's faces looking forward
What have they seen of life yet?

Will one day they all recount
How they passed each waking hour?
Maybe their dreams will all come true
Or maybe they will ever rue.

What wonders of the firmament
We see before us every day
How can man but aspire
As he sits down by the fire?

Each tiny insect flitting by
Its heart beats out as if to cry
That man has treated nature so
He says it is that he might sow!

If we can one day but sit back
And all our peoples learn the knack
To pass by on life's way
And not all men aghast say nay.

The beauty of the country in my heart
Will never from this place depart
All my friends of fur and feather
Their owners must all be clever.

G Buckland-Evers

WONDER OF LIFE

This wonderful world we live in today
Although there is trouble everywhere
The wonders of our Lord we can say
He died for us all our sins to bare

There are wars and turmoil and lots of strife
It's having effect on everyone's life
But our dear heavenly Father up above
Guides and protects us by His love.

He provides our food the sunshine and rain,
And if we trust in Him so much we can gain
Just be a witness and follow the Lord
Become a Christian keep reading His word.

Never forsake Him in work or in play
He watches us all on our holiday
The world's full of riches that we may possess
By loving our Saviour put yourselves to the test.

For His promises and riches are worth more than gold
Look at all the treasures of earth He has to unfold
The flowers, trees, the woodlands for us all to share
He provides for us always year after year

We go on our holidays near or afar
God keeps us safe each and every hour
Abide by His scriptures day after day
Always helping others come what may.

There are none of us perfect but all fully blessed
By the love of our Lord Jesus who puts us all to the test
He died for us all our sins to forgive
So trust love and worship Him as long as you live.

Vi

THE BUTTERFLY

O thou of transient life and delicate art
With pollen-dusted antennae clinging
Tremulously to that half-blown rose's fragrant heart
And your gossamer outspanned wings basking
In the warm summer sun. Fly not away oh faint-
hearted one. If only thou could'st tell me
Why for so short a stay some caring hand did paint
Such fragile wings in perfect symmetry?

Eileen Jackman

I SEE I SEE

I see the moon
I see the stars
And hope one day to visit Mars
To explore the place
And find its green men
Before coming home safely again.

I see the moon
I see the stars
Dream of black holes
And planets afar
Where there could be life
Just like on earth
But if they came
Would we be hurt.

I see the moon
I see the stars
But cannot see God
Or any motor cars
Nor how angels get about
Once God has spoken
About his early doubts.

Keith L Powell

INFORMATION

We hope you have enjoyed reading this book - and that you will continue to enjoy it in the coming years.

If you like reading and writing poetry drop us a line, or give us a call, and we'll send you a free information pack.

Write to

Triumph House Information
1-2 Wainman Road
Woodston
Peterborough
PE2 7BU